D1021949

*Dark Night of the Soul*

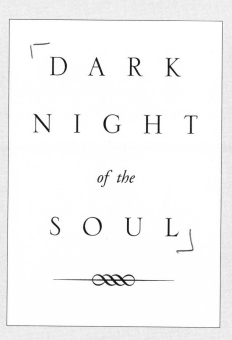

# DARK

# NIGHT

*of the*

# SOUL

SAINT JOHN OF THE CROSS

*New translation and introduction by Mirabai Starr*

RIVERHEAD BOOKS
a member of Penguin Putnam Inc. • New York
2002

Riverhead Books
a member of
Penguin Putnam Inc.
375 Hudson Street
New York, NY 10014

Library of Congress Cataloging-in-Publication Data

John of the Cross, Saint, 1542–1591.
[Noche oscura del alma. English]
Dark night of the soul / by Saint John of the Cross;
new translation and introduction by Mirabai Starr.
p.   cm.
ISBN 1-57322-205-4
1. Mysticism—Spain.   2. Mysticism—Catholic Church.
3. Catholic Church—Doctrines.   I. Title.
BV5080.J77572   2002                    2001-048199
248.2'2—dc21

Printed in the United States of America
1   3   5   7   9   10   8   6   4   2

This book is printed on acid-free paper. ∞

*Book design by Debbie Glasserman*

*I dedicate this translation to the loving memory
of my daughter Jenny Starr, 9/2/87–10/30/01, and my father,
Ian Starr.*

# ACKNOWLEDGMENTS

To all my friends and relations who have guided and upheld me on this path, my loving thanks, especially: Susanna Starr, Amy Starr, Roy Starr, Jenny Starr, Daniela Starr, Kali Little, Jenny Bird, Adair Ferdon, Bobbi Shapiro, and Sean Murphy. To my dear writing group, thank you all.

To my cherished mentors, Charlene McDermott and Natalie Goldberg, perpetual gratitude. To Fr. William Hart McNichols, Fr. Iain Matthew, Fr. Thomas Keating, and to Tim Farrington, profound appreciation for casting such clarity on the heart of Christian mysticism.

Also, I owe a debt of gratitude to the brilliant work of translators E. Allison Peers, and Kieran Kavanaugh and Otilio Rodriguez.

Thanks to my literary agent, Peter Rubie. Thanks to my editor at Riverhead, Amy Hertz, who required no translation to share the vision. Special thanks to Lorie Levison for her insightful reading of the manuscript.

Finally, my deepest appreciation goes to my beloved Ganga Das, whose vast generosity and inner quiet made this work possible.

# CONTENTS

# FOREWORD

*Thomas Moore*

It's common today to hear people say that they're going through a dark night of the soul. As is often the case, many people know the title of John of the Cross's classic without having read a word of it. This new translation should invite people into a book that spells out, in sparkling clear language and structure, certain phases in the spiritual life and the meaning of painful periods of setback and disillusionment.

We all have our ups and downs. At the end of struggles people sometimes claim that they have gone through an ordeal and have come out happy on the other side. One senses a degree of pride in the accomplishment. But I'm not convinced that these victories signal the kind of darkness John describes so carefully. Many spiritual guides warn that we can play tricks on ourselves, bolstering a fragile ego with the thought that we have triumphed in a major rite of passage. The difference lies in the congratulatory attitude: "Look at me—I've succumbed and survived."

Certain challenges have the potential of initiating a person into a new level of experience, but not all painful transitions qualify as a dark night of the soul. It's tempting to bless a difficult period with the awesome phrase, allowing an escape from what is truly a spiritual crisis. Often what we think is the great challenge of a lifetime is only a decoy disguising the real place of transformation. A person may be faced with a difficult marriage and deal with it by escaping into the rigors of a spiritual practice. The dark night, a source of profound change in character, may be at home, while the focus of attention is at the ashram or church.

John of the Cross clearly places the dark night of the soul in the spiritual life, but, from my point of view, spirit and soul need not be separated. Spiritual processes are usually at work beneath and beyond the psychological ones. I don't want to separate these two dimensions, saying that the dark night happens during meditation, while the deep soul is undergoing its changes in ordinary life. But if that is so, how do we distinguish between depression, say, and the dark night John describes?

The key is to distinguish between the ego and the soul. The ego, of course, is the subjective world of the self, the concern of modern psychology and self-help books. Psychology helps us adjust to a difficult world, deal with passions and emotions, and clear the personality for what it might call good functioning. The soul is vast in comparison and full of mysteries. It ranges from the high mysticism of contemplation and vision to deep struggles with meaning and connection.

As I see it, John of the Cross is speaking of mysterious developments in the vast realm of the soul, which includes the psychological. He considers the emotions in relation to spiritual developments. We tend to see difficult feelings as a form of illness, which we hope to conquer, cure, and expel. He has a far greater imagination of human life: his goal is not health but union with the divine.

Here we run into trouble: Do you have to be a Christian to benefit from John's guidance? Do you have to believe in God? On both counts I would say no. Everyone has a spiritual life, even those whose ultimate concern has been deflected into money, sex, drink, or success. John's analysis applies to the human condition, not to a class of believers. On the question of God, to appreciate John's insights it would help to have a subtle idea of the divine. Without dissolving God into vague notions of a supreme power or the Force being with you, it's possible to allow a sense of the infinite and the unknowable in an intelligent philosophy of life. Such an appreciation of the divine might allow us to read this as a book about transcendence, not merely psychological development.

Do you have to be deeply involved in a spiritual practice to experience John's dark night of the soul? I think we're all called to be mystics and that the ladder of emotions John describes may be part of anyone's life. The culture in which we live, for all its religions and spiritual movements, is not inherently religious and so convinces most people that the meaning of life is financial and psychological. But in the very heart of a career decision, a painful divorce, or the memory of abuse lie questions of meaning and value. In those emotional crucibles spiritual issues are being forged. If we had the imagination for it, we would see that every day we are dealing with our spiritual processes. If we could see deeply enough into ordinary life, we might understand what John is writing about.

While I wouldn't equate the dark night with depression, I do think our depressive moods could be imagined spiritually rather than only psychologically. John might help us see that what we call depression is a kind of initiation rather than just an emotional problem. Usually we use the word "depression" for its clinical overtones, suggesting that it is a concern of health and that it can be treated. With John of the Cross in mind, we might imagine the same experience as a crossroads in our effort to make a meaningful life and to achieve a sense of union with the life coursing through us.

Depression has its physical, emotional, and psychological dimensions and is tied in with our background, personality, and experiences. It has its chemical and genetic base. But it is also spiritual and potentially valuable in making a meaningful life. John distinguishes between the dark night of the senses and that of the higher soul. He accounts for both, the deep soul and the high spirit, and he offers a sophisticated map through the full range of this darkness.

Maybe John is right in saying that only a few reach the high levels of this process, but I would still argue that everyone, no matter how confused and ill-situated in life, can have at least modest mystical experiences. They may be as simple as the beautiful stillness that settles at the sight of a sunset or a brief period of wonder at the birth of a child. Mysticism doesn't have to be a life profession. Further, I think that much of our depression, anxiety, and addiction has to do with what John writes about: the soul's need and longing for transcendence. This need is instinctual and unavoidable.

Being engaged in a process of spiritual refinement, the kind John and other mystics chart with close attention to detail, has everything to do with how we feel and how well we deal with life. Spirit and soul are distinct but inseparable. I hope this classic text will help reintroduce the spiritual into our everyday lives. Without it we lack the vision to deal with our personal and social problems effectively and make sense out of a mysterious and challenging existence.

All my life I have wanted to be a translator, partly because I enjoy working with words, but also because I find bad translations an unnecessary obstacle to some of the world's great literature. And so, I am grateful for Mirabai Starr's fluid, inviting translation of this important text. Her translation allows me to adapt John's words to my life with an immediacy I've never felt before in relation to this work. With this marvelous English version in hand, and with the idea that the book speaks about our daily, if hidden, attempts at transcendence, readers might discover their spiritual calling here and make the all-important shift from curing the personality to caring for the soul.

# PREFACE

## MY FRIENDSHIP WITH THE SAINT

When I first encountered the sixteenth-century mystic John of the Cross, he was introduced to me as Spain's favorite poet and most confusing theologian. I loved him immediately. "I've never had a student who really *got* John of the Cross," my venerable old professor of Spanish literature, Sabine Ulibarri, remarked. He shook his head sadly, cocking one eye toward me. What could he mean by that? Here was a man who for decades had been teaching a vibrant classic text overflowing with mystical devotion telling me his students didn't respond. There must be a trick, I mused. I feel like I see John clearly. It's like he's speaking directly to me, using my own code of paradox and formlessness.

I took Ulibarri's sly comment as a personal challenge, enrolled in graduate school in philosophy, and began my master's studies on *Dark Night of the Soul.* Not only did John's message continue to grow clearer, but I developed an irresistible urge to someday compose a new translation of this mystical masterpiece. I wanted to contribute to making *Dark Night* accessible not only to religious scholars and devout Catholics but to every spiritual seeker who finds her own inner life drying up and dropping into darkness. The temptation to try my hand at rendering a fresh version of *Dark Night* grew stronger as I began to assign the classic translations of the text in the college humanities courses I taught.

In the blank wall of my students' faces, I could see the same resistance my old professor had lamented years earlier. I had to work hard to awaken their excitement for this work that meant so much to me. It's not that the two existing English translations were inadequate; on the contrary. Their authors, E. Allison Peers, and Kieran Kavanaugh with Otilio Rodriguez, created eminent renditions of the sacred prose. Yet their unwavering faithfulness to literal accuracy and their identification with the Church yielded somewhat ponderous and slow-moving treatises, preserving much of the obscurity of the Renaissance original. While precise, they are not especially readable.

For years, I held this inspiration in silence. I was busy trying to work out my own practice, parent my children, teach college, and write fiction. The translation project felt like a personal indulgence I was compelled to resist.

Though I resonate strongly with the medieval mystics

and the Desert Fathers and Mothers, I am not a Catholic. I was born into a nonreligious Jewish family that seemed to unconsciously identify itself with that post-Holocaust generation that had given up on God in the wake of the unspeakable atrocities of Nazi Germany. I spent my teens and twenties in ashrams chanting to Hindu goddesses, watching my breath in Buddhist zendos and stupas, prostrating to Allah with the Sufis, and purifying myself in Native American sweat lodges. But eventually, the juice drained out of my spiritual practices and the fireworks faded. By the time I reached my thirties, nothing remained but a quiet connection to emptiness.

Out of that core of stillness, the seed planted long ago by John germinated and pushed up toward the light. I could resist no longer and embarked upon what has become not only a project of literary translation but a journey of personal transformation as well. I see now that any notion of engaging with such powerful teachings without surrendering myself to them is naive. The deeper I stepped into the landscape of the text, the more powerful was the inexplicable sadness to which I woke each morning, and yet the more profound the stillness that seemed to spread itself inside me. I had to question myself carefully: Who was I to speak for this enlightened being and assign myself as his personal editor? All I could do was surrender to the muse of darkness and keep showing up with my dictionary.

Many of the Baroque overtones in this translation have

been removed in hopes of highlighting the essential melodic themes. John is a Christian mystic known for using only the lightest of touches when it comes to direct Christian references. These have been minimized still further, not out of disrespect for Christianity—far from it—but because I felt that this way the universality of his wisdom would shine through even more brightly and touch a greater number of souls who walk a path of suffering, no matter what their religious tradition. In the language of Christian mysticism, the soul is feminine, lover, and God is masculine, Beloved. In the Spanish language, the soul, *el alma,* is also feminine. Regardless of the physical gender of the seeker we are talking about, the pronoun "she" is used throughout the text to identify the spiritual self in love with God; this is a linguistic convention I chose to preserve.

My own spiritual journey began with a passionate longing for God and has led me through the gardens and fires of each of the world's religious traditions, where I followed and was often disappointed by a host of teachers. The expression of my devotion has moved inward now. Sometimes I wonder if this simple emptiness is enough. Lacking the trappings of ceremony and even words, is it truly a spiritual path anymore? This is not always a comfortable state. And yet it is one that I am certain I share with a vast circle of Western seekers. There is a scattered tribe of souls who started out on their journey long ago with all that same fire and find themselves now back *in* the world but definitely not *of* it, wondering if any of it is real—interpersonal relationships, stewardship of the environment, divine union in love with God—and their wondering causes a profound and nameless ache in their hearts.

These are the companions of the spirit I held in my heart as I composed this translation of *Dark Night of the Soul.*

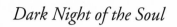

*Dark Night of the Soul*

# INTRODUCTION

## SAYING "YES" TO GOD

Say when you were very young the veil lifted just enough for you to glimpse the underlying Real behind it and then dropped again. Maybe it never recurred, but you could not forget. And this discovery became the prime mover of the rest of your life, in ways you may not have even noticed.

Say you have explored a multitude of spiritual paths. Maybe you have been the embodiment of devotion within each. You perform more austere austerities. Your attention to liturgy is so pointed that you *become* sacred language. You meditate into the small of the night. Your breath grows so gentle that it can scarcely be detected.

Say these practices fill your heart. They make you *feel* holiness like wind through every fiber of your being and *think* rivers of holy thoughts. You recognize the communities they bring you to as your own lost tribe. You get very good at being a Sufi or a Taoist, a contemplative Christian or a yogini. The passion of your love for God intensifies.

Say that while each of the world's great spiritual traditions may hint at that vastness you have longed for, none of them returns you to its threshold. Each of your chosen paths is about *something,* when all you've ever meant to choose is *nothing.* Simply because this is where you first saw God: in the emptiness.

Say prayer starts to dry up on your tongue. Sacred literature becomes fallen leaves, blows away. Meditation brings no serenity anymore. Devotion grows brittle, cracks. The God you bow down to no longer draws you.

Say you bow down anyway. You repeat your mantra along the line of your prayer beads, continue chanting the divine names, melodious. You reread the scriptures, go to mass. You find satisfaction in none of these, yet you persevere. Why not? The things of the world are no competition. You long ago lost interest in material gain, in social status, in interpersonal drama. This wretched limbo lasts for years.

Say each of the familiar spiritual rooms you go to seeking refuge are dark now, and empty. You sit down anyway. You take off your clothes at the door and enter naked. All agendas have fallen away. You grow so still in your nondoing that you forget for a moment that you *are* or that maybe God is *not.* This quietude deepens in proportion to your surrender.

Say what's secretly going on is that the Beloved is loving you back. That your first glimpse of the Absolute was God's first great gift to you. That your years of revelation inside his many vessels was his second gift, wherein, like a mother, he was holding you, like a child, close to his breast, tenderly feeding you. And that this darkness of the soul you have come upon and cannot seem to come out of is his final and greatest gift to you.

Because it is only in this vast emptiness that he can enter, as your Beloved, and fill you. Where the darkness is nothing but unutterable radiance.

Say he knows you are ready to receive him and to be annihilated in love.

Can you say YES to that?

A LIFE OF FIRE

On his deathbed at the age of forty-nine, as the Last Rites were being administered and the appropriate sacred texts recited, John of the Cross interrupted. "Please," he begged his friends, "read to me from the Song of Songs." It is the passion of the lover longing for union with the Beloved, expressed so lyrically in the Songs of Solomon, that characterizes John's entire spiritual journey. It was the ultimate transfiguration of self in God for which John had been waiting all his life and to which he endeavored to gently guide all the souls in his care. To achieve that sweetest of goals, John had walked through unspeakable darkness.

John of the Cross was born John de Yepes y Alvarez in 1542, in the small town of Fontiveros, Spain. Haunted by abject poverty, his family wandered from place to place seeking their livelihood. As an adolescent, John found work at a hospital where people with syphilis came to die. John tended these patients with the depth of compassion that imbued all his relationships from then on. During this time, John was befriended by a Carmelite priest who, deeply impressed by the young man's fine mind and gentle spirit, arranged for him to be sponsored to study theology at the famous University of Salamanca. This required that John join the Carmelite Order. Inexorably drawn to a spiritual path, John enthusiastically agreed.

But monastic life was disappointing. The purity of prayer he craved was obscured by the blind adherence to the ritual and dogma of the institutionalized Church. Disillusioned by the trappings and yearning for direct experience, the young priest seriously considered dropping out of the Order and going into seclusion, where he could devote himself to undistracted contemplation of the divine.

But then the paths of John of the Cross and St. Teresa of Avila crossed. The flame that she was recognized the flame that he was and the resulting conflagration quietly changed the world.

On a practical level, the dynamic fifty-two-year-old nun was busy trying to reform the Carmelite Order. When she first encountered the twenty-five-year-old priest, Teresa immediately recognized in him a profound quality of sanctity coupled with clear vision. Here was a man yearning for the same life of simple contemplation that she was struggling to win back, a devout Carmelite disillusioned by an institution that had lost its holy inspiration. Teresa named John confessor to the nuns in her first reformed convent. Their mutual admiration grew to adoration, and they spent the rest of their lives in passionate spiritual partnership. The mystical poetry of the twelfth-century Sufi saint, Jalaluddin Rumi, reflects a similar connection: the dervish Shams'i'Tabriz was Rumi's living spiritual inspiration.

Teresa's movement became known as the Discalced Carmelite Order, meaning the "Barefoot Carmelites." The monks and nuns took off their shoes and put on rough sandals in honor of the stark simplicity to which they were striving to return. While King Philip of Spain fully supported the reform, officials in Rome were antagonistic. John paid for his participation in this effort. In 1577, at the age of thirty-five, he was captured by a group of friars committed to upholding the traditions of the established Church. He was taken to Toledo where he was interrogated and tortured. They tried to force him into denouncing the reform, but he refused. And so he was imprisoned in a tiny dark closet that had previously served as a toilet. He was brought out only to be flogged in the center of the dining commons while the monks ate their dinner.

John himself suffered virtual starvation. That first winter, he endured brutal cold and was offered neither cloak nor blanket. In the summer, the heat was stifling and his clothes began to rot on his body. At first he took comfort in his quiet interior connection to God, but over time the divine presence began to fade and John could not help but wonder if his Beloved had abandoned him. He was Jonah languishing inside the belly of the whale.

In the depths of his despair, John composed passionate love poems to God. Since he had no access to writing materials, he committed them to memory. Finally, a Carmelite brother assigned to guard the prisoner, who basked daily in the saint's serene yet passionate presence, secretly procured a scroll, a quill, and some ink, allowing John to surreptitiously scribble his verses in the darkness. Although his creative flow saved his sanity, it could not save his life. Convinced after nine months that if he endured another moment of incarceration he would die, John tied knots in scraps of cloth and slipped through a tiny window at the upper edge of his cell. He lowered himself down the long wall of the monastery and into the safety of the night. He found shelter in a nearby convent of Teresa's nuns, where he crept through the gate, leaned his head against the archway of the chapel, and wept as the sisters recited the Angelus.

After his miraculous escape from prison, John fell into a state of profound ecstasy. He had traveled through perfect darkness and emerged to find the living God waiting for him in the depths of his own heart. The communion between lover and Beloved yielded a permanent transformation in the God-intoxicated man. At the height of this mystical state, John composed the poem "Songs of the Soul: One Dark Night." Later, he described it as "an outpouring of love for God," which he was powerless to resist. Like the

Songs of Solomon, John's verses sang of the passion of long-ing and the ecstasy of secret union with the Beloved—a union that could take place only after the soul had made her escape from the confines of her old house through the wil-derness of the darkest night.

Although the poem is a metaphor for the spiritual jour-ney, it reads more like sublime erotica than acceptable the-ology. And so John's Discalced Brethren gently prevailed upon him to write a commentary on his mystical verses. This gave rise to the brilliant spiritual treatise known as *Dark Night of the Soul.*

For the next two decades John dedicated himself to the necessary evil of administrating the reform, which spread all over Spain, and to the sweet simplicity of guiding the spiri-tual lives of his Barefoot Sons and Daughters. He continued to compose love poems to God and to write theological commentaries on them. Drawn to alleviate suffering wher-ever he encountered it, John was known for his gentle kind-ness and childlike playfulness. Although the doctrine of the dark night is harsh and uncompromising, the priest, it seems, could not bear to see anybody sad or sick. He was as likely to gather the monks for a hike up into the Andalucian hills to contemplate their God under the open night sky as to call them to the confessional.

As the years unfolded, John grew less and less at home in the world. His silent raptures would last for hours. He was continuously struggling to call himself back down to the business at hand while all his soul wanted was to float upwards in loving contemplation of the divine. Conversations with Teresa would begin with passionate declarations of the greatness of God and end in rapt silence in which both of them became transfixed by the glory they had been extolling.

Toward the end of the saint's life, envies and disquietudes within the reform itself led to a secret effort to remove him from the sphere of influence. John was about to be sent to the New World—a mission to which he willingly consented—when an old leg wound, suffered in prison two decades earlier, became suddenly infected and spread to his back. His Superior insisted that he receive medical attention and gave him two options: to seek care in the convent of Baeza where the nuns adored him, or to travel to the monastery of Ubeda where no one knew him.

True to his humble nature, John chose Ubeda. The Prior there, a bitter man who had heard stories of the sick priest's lifelong sanctity, took an immediate disliking to him. He savagely neglected John's care, complaining of the costs the patient exacted from his operating budget. John's condition grew worse. When John felt that his death was approaching, he called the Prior to him so that he could apologize for all the trouble he had caused. Struck by the dying saint's radiance, the Prior was overcome by remorse. He, in turn, begged forgiveness of John and the heart-opening he experienced that day irrevocably changed him.

That night, John's closest Discalced Brethren found their way to his side and gathered around him in a circle of love.

Filled with the poetry of divine love, he died whispering the words of the Psalmist: "Into your hands, Beloved, I commend my spirit."

Forty years after his death, the first complete edition of John's writings was published. Ninety-five years later, he was canonized by Pope Benedict XIII. It was not until the middle of the twentieth century that John of the Cross was officially named patron of Spanish poets. Unlike his beloved friend and mentor, St. Teresa of Avila, John was not a charismatic character. In fact, his lifetime was characterized by a series of excruciating misunderstandings. His small stature and quiet nature rendered him nearly invisible; if it weren't for Teresa's constant efforts to draw attention to his spiritual mastery, he may well have died in simple obscurity.

John's passion was reflected in his writing. Yet, the same poetry that brought comfort and inspiration to the monks and nuns in his care drew the dangerous attention of the Inquistion, which eventually destroyed him. From the tightrope of renegade spirituality, John might just as easily have tumbled into persecution for heresy as canonization for sainthood.

Even now, John is little known outside of Spain or beyond the confines of academic and theological studies. Many people toss around the term "dark night of the soul" in reference to a period of personal pain arising from a bad divorce or a career catastrophe. Few people are familiar with John as the articulator of a brilliant and penetrating teaching on love and emptiness.

## "I AM NOTHING"

In a Western world busy recovering from a legacy of shame and blame, John's continual declaration that "I am nothing" (and the implicit suggestion that we, too, are nothing) may set off alarms. But these would be false alarms. The radical humility John speaks of has little to do with the pathology of self-deprecation. It is a state of blessedness, where we let go of identification with the small, separate self so that we can rest in our togetherness with the Beloved. To be truly humble is to feel a tender acceptance of all reality just as it is, which includes compassion for ourselves just as we are. This kind of humility is a surrender of our whole being to the simple truth of love.

In the dark night, says John, the secret essence of the soul that knows the truth is calling out to God: Beloved, you pray, please remind me again and again that I am nothing. Strip me of the consolations of my complacent spirituality. Plunge me into the darkness where I cannot rely on any of my old tricks for maintaining my separation. Let me give up on trying to convince myself that my own spiritual deeds are bound to be pleasing to you. Take all my juicy spiritual feelings, Beloved, and dry them up, and then please light them on fire. Take my lofty spiritual concepts and plunge them into darkness, and then burn them. Let me only love you, Beloved. Let me quietly and with unutterable simplicity just love you.

This humility is not fatalism. It is active and impassioned.

John would likely distrust some of today's self-proclaimed spiritual teachers who make a living preaching a path of comfort and ease, who declare themselves perfected beings, who make of enlightenment a commodity accessible to the privileged, who adopt spirituality as a style, who claim that there is some pot of gold to be collected at the end of the rainbow. The true teachers are often the invisible ones.

The dark night is not an abstract notion on some list of spiritual experiences every seeker is supposed to have. The dark night descends on a soul only when everything else has failed. When you are no longer the best meditator in the class because your meditation produces absolutely nothing. When prayer evaporates on your tongue and you have nothing left to say to God. When you are not even tempted to return to a life of worldly pleasure because the world has proven empty and yet taking another step through the void of the spiritual life feels futile because you are no good at it and it seems that God has given up on you, anyway.

This, says John, is the beginning of blessedness. This is the choiceless choice when the soul can do nothing but surrender. Because even if you cannot sense a shred of the Beloved's love for you, even if you can scarcely conjure up your old passion for him, it has become perfectly clear that you are incapable of doing anything on your own to remedy your spiritual brokenness. All efforts to purge your unspiritual inclinations have only honed the laser of attention on the false self. Unwilling to keep struggling, the soul finds itself surrendering to its deepest inner wound and breathing in the stillness there.

"The central paradox of the spiritual path," says Tim Farrington, author of *Hell of Mercy*, "is that in striving to transcend the self, we actually build it up. Our holy solutions invariably calcify into grotesque casts of ego. The dark night is God's solution to our solutions, dissolving our best-laid constructions anew into the mystery of grace. It happens in spite of our best efforts to resist it. But thank God it happens."

The only action left to the soul, ultimately, is to put down its self-importance and cultivate a simple loving attention toward the Beloved. That's when the Beloved takes over and all our holy intentions vaporize. That's when the soul, says John, is infused passively with his love. Though his radiance is imperceptible to the faculty of the senses and invisible to the faculty of the intellect, the soul that has allowed itself to be empty can at last be filled and overflow with him.

Humility, then, is not a matter of beating ourselves up. It is not a question of judging ourselves as stupid or sinful, as hopeless and bad. Who are we to judge these things? Humility, for John, is the gentle acceptance of that most tender place inside ourselves that throbs with the pain of separation from the Beloved. It is that deep knowingness that identification with the false self brings nothing but further separation. It is an initially reluctant dropping down into the emptiness and an ultimate experience of peace when we stop doing and rediscover simple being. It is the Sabbath of the soul when we heed the call to cease creating and remember that we are created.

## SUCHNESS

The emptiness of the dark night is a yielding emptiness. It is an emptiness that gives way to the fullness of all possibility, which manifests as limitless diversity, which circles back to emptiness. It is the impossible-to-translate *sunyata* of Buddhism. It is the living substratum of all reality. It is rooted in quiet.

"God spoke only one word for all eternity and he spoke it in silence," says John, "and it is in eternal silence that we hear it." Plunged at some point into the darkness of the spiritual journey, where all preconceptions of holiness are obliterated, we have nowhere to go but into the silence where the divine reality secretly reveals itself to a consciousness cleared of the ongoing chatter of the false self. What the Buddhists call the "monkey mind" eventually settles down so that sacred truth can speak itself.

This is where contemplative practice bears fruit. The contemplatives show us that by learning to be in stillness, we can access "the divine word spoken in silence," the secret word that sets up the vibration from which all creation issues. By sitting quietly with the breath, the blessed "no-self" begins to emerge.

In an article on Carmelite prayer, Fr. Iain Matthew says

that contemplation "commits a person to complete confidence and trust in the love of God who is continually breaking into our lives. The contemplative stance is an openness to that love and the demands it makes on us to change. To be a contemplative is to be a watch in the night for the approach of Mystery. And it is a readiness to be transformed in an engagement with that Mystery."

Fr. Thomas Keating, known for the practice of "centering prayer," says that when John talks about being nothing, what he means is that by relinquishing any fixed point of reference for the false self, we can let down into an ever-deepening identification with God. Far from reflecting the shame of our own unworthiness, this detachment from our individuality allows us to see that having been created in the image of God is to be perfectly beautiful and perfectly good. In contemplative stillness, attachment to our own limitations begins to fall away so that we can participate in the unspoken holiness that gives rise to all that is.

If all your spiritual activities have grown empty and you are compelled to walk away, says John, tie yourself to one practice only: contemplative silence. Abandon discursive prayer if it has become mechanical and meaningless. Let go of holy images if they no longer evoke the sacred. Refrain from spiritual discourse if it tastes like idle gossip in your mouth. But do not turn away from the silence.

It's tempting to give up the spiritual journey when the darkness falls. It's easy to get bogged down by cynicism and cease reaching out for the Beloved. But contemplative practice, Fr. Keating points out, keeps us alert to the movements of the false self and makes a small space for us to hear the invitation to enter into the ultimate reality, which is nothing other than God's love for us. "This whole thing is God's idea!" Fr. Keating exclaims. John would agree.

This is a path of annihilation of the ego. But we must first be brought home to ourselves before we can bear to see our nothingness before God. It is not an optimal journey for the seeker whose selfhood has been so badly wounded and diminished that the only sensible course is one of healing and building up a strong ego. It is not an appropriate teaching for those who suffer from a chronic need for affirmation. It is less for those who are struggling to find themselves than it is for the ones who have a clear sense of self and are ready to purify it. Radical humility, John teaches, is not a malady requiring a cure but the blessing of the "yes" that rises from the very core of the soul in love with God.

And yet neither is the dark night reserved for some spiritual elite whose personalities are so strong and intact that they can afford to blithely cast them into the flames of union. Someone who is broken, says Fr. Matthew, who has struggled all his life with some intense deficiency, may have a uniquely powerful relationship with God. Fr. Matthew suggests that these teachings can throw out a lifeline to all who suffer. This is a path for those who use their suffering as a tool for transformation. In the dark night of each soul, we are simultaneously annihilated and immeasurably strengthened.

## SAYING "NO" TO GOD

Fr. Matthew describes evil as the saying of an absolute "no" to God. Sin, then, would be any act that engages the "no." Perhaps hell, then, is the consequence of the "no" in the life of the soul trapped in denial of God. And the devil might simply be that aspect of our selves that most stubbornly refuses God.

In this translation, all references to evil, sin, hell, and the devil, as states and entities, have been replaced with terms that reflect a false sense of separation from God. If the divine is truly divine and ultimate reality truly ultimate, then there is nothing but God. Where John spoke of *El Diablo,* the term "fragmented self" has been chosen to describe that shadow side of our own being so lost in the illusion of separation from the Beloved that all it can do is rebel against merging. The terms "Spirit of Evil" and the "Fallen One" evoke the perils that result from this delusion.

*Islam* means "the peace that comes with utter surrender to God." The primary declaration of Muslims is "There is no God but God." The first part of this prayer is negation: there is no God. But it is only out of this absolute emptiness that the affirmation of truth can rise: but *God.* The fragmented self John calls *El Diablo* can be seen as that aspect of our being that has become disoriented by the negation and has lost the thread of the affirmation.

It is the fragmented self that is terrified of annihilation.

And with good reason. Its suspicion is well-founded that if it were to allow the soul to follow through with its intentions and attain union with the Beloved, the result would be its own death. The soul cannot enter into the fusion of divine love with its shadow clinging to its skirt. It must strip itself of identification with the small self and step naked into the garden where the Beloved is waiting.

The closer the soul approaches on its journey home to God, the more ferocious is the resistance of the fragmented self. Divine union is about wholeness, and the fragmented self does not want to be made whole. But because only God is real, the "no" ultimately disappears in the radiance of divine love like a broken heart that heals the instant the dreamer wakes in the night to feel the arms of her true love holding her close, just as he has always held her.

## THE JOURNEY OF LOVE

The road to the divine encounter is not for the weekend adventurer. It will quickly disappoint the spiritually curious. If you crave ecstatic visions and spiritual comforts, do not bother to walk this way. The dark night of the soul is for the seeker so on fire with love for God that she will get to him by any means necessary. This includes being willing to plunge into the abyss of the Unknown, of the Unknowable. It is a path for the spiritually desperate. And yet it is a state over which the soul has absolutely no control.

Before the soul even begins this journey, she will already have suffered acute disillusionment with the world. Plagued by an unquenchable thirst for the sacred, she has lost interest in material security and social recognition. She has dedicated herself to the cultivation of spiritual practice. Her only hope is that by blowing on the coals of intuition of the divine with the breath of prayer, it will burst into flames and reveal the Beloved. But the spiritual life turns out to be not at all what she thought it would be. The radiance she anticipated looks exactly like impenetrable darkness.

John describes this darkness as being of two kinds, which correspond to the two aspects of the human soul: the sensory and the spiritual. And so there are two successive nights: the night of sense and the night of spirit. In the night of sense, the soul is stripped of all *perceptions* of God. In the night of spirit, all *ideas* of God fall away.

Early in her spiritual life, the soul could not help but wallow like a happy baby in the juicy feelings evoked by spiritual practices. In the night of sense, these juices dry up and the soul is left baffled and bereft. This, John assures us, is a good thing. It means that God sees that we have grown strong enough to endure a light burden of aridity. He has removed us from the spiritual breast and set us down on our own tender feet.

Many souls lose faith at this point. They conclude that they must not be suited to the spiritual life and they give up. They have mistaken a state of purity for an impoverished one. Yet there is no question of returning their energies to the world, which has lost any allure. And so they engage halfheartedly in spiritual practice, resigned to aridity, coming to some small peace with emptiness.

Every once in a while, the tree of prayer, which had been long dormant, bursts into blossom and the seeker feels momentarily connected to the divine sweetness he has always craved. Maybe someone he loves is dying, and he slips into the hospital chapel to call out for God. Or a sunset or a kiss or a sleeping infant may rend a hole in the curtain of illusion, and he glimpses the perfect beauty of the Grand Design behind it all. The winds of sensory purgation soon blow back through, however, and the garden is again laid bare. The soul sits helpless amid the spiritual wreckage and simply breathes in the darkness. There is nothing else to do. The seeker in this state may be shy about disclosing his inner struggle to anyone for fear it will reveal nothing but his own deadly doubts and spiritual failures.

The soul who perseveres without the motivation of sensory satisfaction moves beyond what John refers to as the state of the beginner and into the state of the adept. This is the dreadful night of the spirit, where not only is the soul denuded of divine feelings but any ability to conceptualize the Beloved collapses. The seeker is confronted with the terror of formlessness.

Where the night of sense requires some active participation on the soul's part, in the night of spirit God takes over. In fact, John warns, any effort the seeker might make to further his spiritual progress not only fails to produce results but might actually hinder the work the Beloved is secretly executing deep inside the soul. All the seeker can do is surrender to the darkness and take humble refuge in the ineffable stillness of what Fr. Iain calls the soul's "spiritual meltdown."

The soul in the dark night cannot, by definition, understand what is happening to her. Accustomed to feeling and conceiving of the Beloved her own way, she does not realize that the darkness is a blessing. She perceives God's gentle touch as an unbearable burden. She feels miserable and unworthy, convinced that God has abandoned her, afraid she may herself be turning against him. In her despair, the soul does not recognize that God is teaching her in a secret way now, a way with which the faculties of sense and reason cannot interfere.

At the same time that the soul in the night of spirit becomes paralyzed in spiritual practice, her love-longing for God begins to intensify. In the stillness left behind by its broken-open senses and intellect, a quality of abundance starts to grow inside the emptied soul. It turns out that the Beloved is longing for union with the lover as fervently as she has been yearning for him. In the night of spirit, he is calling it home to him and, like the song of Krishna's flute luring the *gopi* to the divine embrace, God will whisper to the soul in the depth of darkness and guide it through the wilderness of the Unknown until it is annihilated in the flames of perfect love.

## WHAT NOW?

A life of contemplative devotion could be somewhat easier for the ones who remove themselves from the distractions of the marketplace and set themselves apart in mountaintop monasteries than for those immersed in the world. Monks and nuns may well struggle mightily with their inner shadows, but the focus of their lives is primarily on a direct relationship with ultimate reality.

What about those of us who struggle each day to pay taxes to a government we may not agree with, spending our weeks engaged in labors we may not find fulfilling? Those of us who are called in the night to nurse a sick baby or pick up a rebellious teen from the police station? Those of us so exhausted from a day of chopping our twenty-first-century wood and carrying our twenty-first-century water that the thought of getting up an extra hour earlier each morning to sit in silent meditation feels like adding another ten pounds to our already barely manageable load? What about those of us who spent our youth trying every way we could find to "get to God" and ended up in Cincinnati or Santa Fe, with a couple of failed marriages behind us, ownership of a modest business, and credit card debts for pleasures we cannot remember? Those of us struggling to keep our community water clean and our kids crack-free and our own codependent tendencies in check?

Many of us have reached a plateau and have become resigned to the aridity of our spiritual lives. We are probably caught in the wilderness John calls the "night of sense." We no longer pursue the spiritual fireworks we once found so compelling. The "highs" we used to attain while chanting and prostrating and dancing for God have proven to be fluff obscuring the simple quietude of divine suchness. And yet, there is bitterness and grief in our capitulation. We may no longer be suffering from the delusions of a spiritual carnival, but we have lost something vital.

Maybe what we're missing is the love. Maybe we have forgotten that the only reason to strive and to surrender, to sit in the silence or to make a joyful noise unto the Lord, is because ultimate reality is love, and it is only by loving that we remember. Be still now, John would say. Borrow a moment from each day to stop and touch down with the stillness that is your true nature, which is God's true nature, which is nothing, which is love.

Perhaps if we recommit to the journey without any hope of arriving anywhere, the longing for union will rekindle and we will be propelled into the terrible night of the spirit where we are simultaneously overcome with thirst for the Beloved and lost in utter formlessness. But then, maybe this night of spirit will make us wish we had been content to hang out in the tolerable aridity of the night of sense where we rarely felt connected to our Beloved but at least we still knew he was there.

Is it enough to do our best to be good citizens of the planet, raising compassionate families and running ecologically responsible businesses, reading meaningful books and guiding friends through authentic crises, showing up for the occasional Dharma talk or celebration of the Shabbat, keeping a framed photo of a Hindu guru or a statue of the Virgen de Guadalupe in our bedroom to honor what we know to be that which, though intangible, is Most Important? Why plunge willingly off this comfortable flat place and into the abyss?

The leap is not required. Most souls never jump, says John. There is no judgment about this. The dark night is not about who wins the race by crossing the finish line of self-annihilation. There is nothing we can do, anyway. The dark night is about being fully present in the tender, wounded emptiness of our own souls. It's about not turning away from the pain but learning to rest in it. Rather than distracting ourselves from the simple darkness at our core, we sit with it, paying close attention, and opening our hearts to all that is left, which is love. It is the cultivation of compassion for our suffering selves and for all selves who suffer the illusion of separation from the Beloved. It a quiet, formless, willingness to return.

### Songs of the Soul

*On a dark night,*
*Inflamed by love-longing—*
*O exquisite risk!—*
*Undetected I slipped away.*
*My house, at last, grown still.*

*Secure in the darkness,*
*I climbed the secret ladder in disguise—*
*O exquisite risk!—*
*Concealed by the darkness.*
*My house, at last, grown still.*

*That sweet night: a secret.*
*Nobody saw me;*
*I did not see a thing.*
*No other light, no other guide*
*Than the one burning in my heart.*

*This light led the way*
*More clearly than the risen sun*
*To where he was waiting for me*
*—The one I knew so intimately—*
*In a place where no one could find us.*

*O night, that guided me!*
*O night, sweeter than sunrise!*
*O night, that joined lover with Beloved!*
*Lover transformed in Beloved!*

*Upon my blossoming breast,*
*Which I cultivated just for him,*
*He drifted into sleep,*
*And while I caressed him,*
*A cedar breeze touched the air.*

*Wind blew down from the tower,*
*Parting the locks of his hair.*
*With his gentle hand*
*He wounded my neck*
*And all my senses were suspended.*

*I lost myself. Forgot myself.*
*I lay my face against the Beloved's face.*
*Everything fell away and I left myself behind,*
*Abandoning my cares*
*Among the lilies, forgotten.*

—John of the Cross
translated by Mirabai Starr

# DARK NIGHT

# OF THE SOUL

*This is a commentary on the* Songs of the Soul.
*It tells of the soul's journey along the
path that leads to perfect union in love with God,
to the extent that she can reach him in this life.
It also describes the qualities of the soul
who has arrived at such perfection.*

## PROLOGUE

We will begin by entirely unfolding the songs of the soul; then we will explore the meaning of the first two verses individually, which describe the effects of the two spiritual purifications: that of senses and that of spirit. The other six proclaim the myriad wonders of spiritual illumination and union in love with God, which are ineffable.

### Noche Oscura (Canciones del Alma)

*En una noche oscura,
con ansias, en amores inflamada,*

*¡oh dichosa ventura!*
*salí sin ser notada,*
*estando ya mi casa sosegada.*

*A oscuras y segura*
*por la secreta escala, disfrazada,*
*¡oh dichosa ventura!*
*a oscuras y en celada,*
*estando ya mi casa sosegada.*

*En la noche dichosa,*
*en secreto, que nadie me veía*
*ni yo miraba cosa,*
*sin otra luz y guía*
*sino la que en el corazón ardía.*

*Aquésta me guiaba*
*más cierto que la luz del mediodía*
*a donde me esperaba*
*quien yo bien me sabía,*
*en parte donde nadie parecía.*

*¡oh noche que guiaste!*
*¡oh noche amable más que la alborada,*
*oh noche que juntaste*
*Amado con amada,*
*amada en el amado transformada!*

*En mi pecho florido*
*que entero para él solo se guardaba,*

*allí quedó dormido*
*y yo le regalaba,*
*y el ventalle de cedros aire daba.*

*El aire de la almena*
*cuando yo sus cabellos esparcía,*
*con su mano serena*
*en mi cuello hería*
*y todos mis sentidos suspendía.*

*Quedéme y olvidéme,*
*el rostro recliné sobre el amado,*
*cesó todo y dejéme,*
*dejando mi cuidado*
*entre las azucenas olvidado.*

*Begins an explanation of the verses which describe*
*the path the soul follows*
*on her journey to union in love with God.*

As we embark on an explanation of these verses, remember that the soul who utters them is speaking from a place of perfection. She has attained absolute union in love with God. She has endured intense tribulations. Through dedicated spiritual practice, she has navigated the steep and slender path of infinite life. This is the way the soul must journey to arrive at such sublime and delicious union with the Beloved. The soul realizes how blessed she is to have passed through such a narrow and restricted route.

And so it is with great joy that she sings in the first verse of her coming to the place of perfect love. She aptly names her perilous journey a "dark night." We will soon see why.

Now the soul, rejoicing in having walked the narrow road which yielded such abundance of blessing, speaks like this . . .

# BOOK I

---∞∞∞---

# NIGHT

*of*

# SENSE

*Explores the dark night of sensory purification.*

*On a dark night,*
*Inflamed by love-longing—*
*O exquisite risk!—*
*Undetected I slipped away.*
*My house, at last, grown still.*

In the first verse, the soul sings of the path she followed as she left behind attachment to herself and to created things. Through radical humility, she has died to her old self. She tells of living a new life—sweet and delicious—in love with God. The soul calls this going forth a "dark night," which is pure contemplation. The negation of the self and of all things unfolds passively within her.

The soul reports that she was able to make her escape through her burning passion for the Beloved, a passion which he himself gave to her within the depths of dark contemplation. She places special value on the joy she has come to know by having walked through this night all the way to

God. Her journey has been so fruitful that not one of the three enemies—the world, the Spirit of Evil, and the animal nature—could possibly impede her passage. The purifying night of contemplation served to muffle the distractions, the hungers, and all the troubling stirrings of the sensual house and lull them to sleep.

And so she begins to sing:

*"On a dark night . . ."*

# CHAPTER 1

‒‒‒‒∞∞∞‒‒‒‒

*Unfolds the first verse and begins to explore
the imperfections of beginners.*

Souls begin to enter this dark night once God draws them
forth from the state of the beginners, who merely muse about
the spiritual path, and places them in the state of the adepts,
the true contemplatives. This is the start of a journey that
will lead to the blessed place of perfection, which is the divine union of the soul with God.

To better understand the nature of this night of the soul
and God's purpose for putting her here, it would be good to
take a look at some of the qualities of the spiritual beginner.
If, by hearing these teachings, beginners recognize their own
fragility, they may take heart and call on God to place them,
please, in this night so that they can be fortified in virtue and
made ready for the unutterable delights of love with God.

Once the soul has completely surrendered to serving God,
she is nurtured and caressed by him, just like a tender baby
with its loving mother. The mother holds the child close in
her arms, warming it with the heat of her breasts, nourish-
ing it with sweet milk and softened foods. But as the baby

grows, the mother gradually caresses it less. She begins to hide her tender love. She sets the child down on its own two feet. This is to help the baby let go of its childish ways and experience more significant things.

The grace of God is just like a loving mother. Grace kindles in the soul renewed warmth and ardor for serving God. Through grace, the soul discovers sweet spiritual milk and effortlessly drinks in all the things of God. Through grace, God gives the soul intense delight in spiritual practices, just as a loving mother places her breast tenderly into the mouth of her child.

And so the soul at first finds her bliss in spending long periods—sometimes whole nights—deep in prayer. Penances are her pleasures. Fasting makes her happy. Participating in rituals and discussing divine things consoles her.

Even though she may tend earnestly to her spiritual practice, the beginner notices that she is spiritually weak and imperfect. This is because she is still motivated to engage in spiritual practices because of the comforts and pleasures they yield. She has not yet been galvanized by the powerful struggle to live the true virtues. A soul only achieves perfection in proportion to the perfect habits she has cultivated. The beginner has not practiced long enough to hone her spiritual skills, so she still works feebly, like a child.

To make sense of the beginner's dangerous attachment to the delights spiritual practices offer, let's take a look, one by one, at the seven imperfections. We will see how spiritual beginners are just like small children.

# CHAPTER 2

*Some of the imperfections of spiritual
pride suffered by beginners.*

Beginners feel such passion about divine things and are so devoted to their spiritual practices! They bask in their bounty.

Even though holiness is in itself humbling, these souls are still imperfect, and so a certain secret pride begins to rise in them. Overly satisfied with themselves and their accomplishments, they develop this vain urge to talk about spiritual things in front of others. Sometimes they presume to teach rather than to learn. In their hearts, they condemn those whose devotion they deem less than adequate; they may even say so out loud. They act like the Pharisee who put down the publican while bragging about himself and praising God for his own good works.

Maybe the fragmented self, caught in the illusion of separation from God and fearing the annihilation of divine union, stirs the soul's fervor for spiritual practice only to try and build up her pride and presumption. Maybe it knows quite well that spiritual accomplishments are not only worthless but can actually become vices.

Sometimes these beginners grow so wicked that they want no one else but themselves to look good. And so they condemn others at every opportunity. They behold the mote in their brother's eye and never notice the log in their own. They reach for another's gnat and swallow their own camel.

Beginners may be so anxious to be recognized and praised that they quickly conclude their spiritual teachers do not understand them when they criticize some element of the beginner's spirit or behavior. They may even judge their teachers to be not spiritual enough. So, they rush off to find some other guide more to their liking, one who will properly congratulate them on their spiritual skills. They flee as if from death from anyone who might try to correct them and lead them to a safe road. They may even become hostile toward such a guide. Ever presumptuous, they resolve many lofty things but do not accomplish much.

Beginners can be so eager for others to notice how spiritual they are that, with the assistance of the fragmented self, they contrive these little displays—sighs and other ceremonies, public raptures rather than private ones—which, to their delight, call special attention to them.

Many yearn to be the favorite of their spiritual teacher and to grow intimate with him. From this desire arises a thousand little envies and disquietudes. They are reluctant to reveal their naked imperfections, apprehensive that their spiritual guide might think bad things about them. They cast a false glow on their deeds to make themselves seem less messy. They go to their guide to excuse rather than to accuse themselves. Sometimes they even seek out another teacher to speak the truth about their wrongs so that their own teacher may believe they have done only pure good.

True humility, of course, would be to make less of their actual goodness in hopes that no one would notice them at all.

While sometimes beginners struggle to hide their faults, other times they grow overly saddened by them. Having begun to believe that they were already saints, they become angry and impatient with themselves when they discover that this is not the case. Self-condemnation is just another imperfection.

Beginners usually yearn for God to take away their faults not for God's sake but for their own peace of mind. What they don't realize is that if God were to liberate them from all these annoyances they would be in even graver danger of pride and presumption. They hate it when others are praised and love it when they are praised themselves. They are like those foolish virgins who sought oil from others when their own lamps went dead! [Mt. 25:8]

Tainted by these early imperfections, some souls go on to intensify them, which is very harmful. Some beginners have more wickedness, some less. Some show small flickers of imperfection which, thankfully, go nowhere. But there is not a beginner, in the fervor of her beginning, who does not fall into some degree of this trouble.

Yet those on the true path to perfection walk in a special way through all this. They are assisted by their very humility, placing little importance on their own efforts and drawing little satisfaction from their accomplishments. They see everyone else as far better than themselves and may suffer some holy envy, longing to serve God as others do.

As their passion for God intensifies, they work harder for him, loving the service they are engaged in. But as their humility deepens, so does their awareness of how much God deserves from them and how inadequate everything they do really is. The more they do, the less satisfied they feel. So vast is their generosity and love toward God that nothing they could possibly offer him seems worthy.

Absorbed, drenched, swept up by this loving anxiety, they do not take any notice of what others are doing or not doing, except insofar as they perceive that others are better than they are. They think little of themselves and only wish that others would dismiss them altogether. Even if others do value them and praise them, they cannot believe a thing they say; such compliments strike them as ridiculous.

With deep tranquility and humility, they yearn to learn from anyone who might have anything to teach them. This is exactly the opposite of those others who always consider themselves to be the teachers, the ones who pluck the words out of the mouth of someone offering some instruction as if they already knew everything.

But these gentle souls, far from pretending to be anyone's teacher, are open to the journey and will set out on a completely different road from the one they have been walking if that is recommended. They never presume to be right about anything.

They do not feel like talking about themselves, even to their spiritual guides, because they consider their religious deeds to be so insignificant that they're not worth mentioning. They are much more interested in discussing their faults and transgressions than their virtues, eager to share whatever is wrong with them. They are inclined to seek direction from people who do not think much of them or of their spiritual accomplishments.

These are qualities of a spirit that is pure and simple and true. And this is what is pleasing to God. The wise spirit of God dwells within them, inspiring them to keep their treasures concealed and reveal only their imperfections. As he denies this grace from the proud, it is bestowed, along with all the other virtues, upon these humble souls.

Such beginners would offer the very blood of their hearts to anyone who loves God. They draw upon everything in themselves to serve those who serve him. Whenever they realize they are falling into imperfection, they bear this with humility, with softness of spirit, with a balance of loving awe of God and deep trust in him.

Very few beginners tread the path so skillfully. Just as few fall into grave error. The dark night will purify them and move them along the road to perfection.

# CHAPTER 3

*Some of the imperfections of spiritual greed
suffered by beginners.*

Many beginners are discontent with the spirituality God has given them. They go around melancholy and petulant because they cannot access the consolation they crave in their spiritual practices. They are greedy.

These are the ones who cannot get enough of listening to spiritual counsels, of studying religious precepts, of acquiring and consuming sacred literature. Their efforts are imbalanced toward these pursuits and away from the simple commitment to cultivating inner poverty of spirit. They load themselves down with exotic images and artifacts. They let go of some only to take on others. They exchange this one for that one, and then they change back again. First they have to have one particular holy object, next a different one. They prefer one string of prayer beads over another because it's fancier. Some gather spiritual relics and amulets like children hoarding trinkets.

All I am condemning is the attachment of the heart to the style, multitude, and intricacy of these objects. This is contrary to the poverty of spirit which concerns itself with nothing but the substance of devotion, which is satisfied with whatever fulfills this simple end, and which tires of multiplicity and ornamentation. True devotion springs from the heart. It is the truth spiritual objects represent that matters. All the rest is mere attachment. For the soul to pass into perfection, such cravings need to fall away.

I knew a person who used a simple cross fashioned from an olive branch and held together with a twisted pin for more than ten years; he carried it with him everywhere. This was a man of no small intelligence or insight. I saw another who prayed with beads made of fish bone; God did not hold her devotion any less precious because of this. It is clear that neither of these objects was of special workmanship or material value.

Those who begin well and progress along their path are the souls who do not attach themselves to visible instruments or burden themselves with acquisitions. They are not interested in knowing more than is necessary to do good works. They set their eyes on God alone, on being right with him. This is their passion! With abundant generosity, they give away all they have. Whether spiritual or temporal possessions, these souls are happy to learn how to live without them, for love of their God and charity to their neighbor. Remember that their eyes are fixed on the inner treasure and that they yearn only to please God and not themselves.

But the soul cannot fully purge herself of any imperfections until God delivers her into the passive purgation of that dark night. Still, to the extent that she possibly can, the soul must strive to purify and perfect herself. In this way, she earns the divine cure, in which God heals the soul of all she could not hope to heal within herself. No matter how hard she tries, the soul cannot by her own active efforts purify herself sufficiently to be in the slightest degree prepared for the divine union of perfect love. God himself takes her hand and purifies her in the dark fire.

# CHAPTER 4

*Some of the imperfections of spiritual*
*lust suffered by beginners.*

Among the imperfections of beginners purged by the dark night is spiritual lust. It is not that the lust is itself spiritual, but it is aroused by spiritual things. Often in practices—utterly beyond her control—impure stirrings will arise and overwhelm the sensual part of the soul. Sometimes this occurs even when she is deep in prayer.

Human nature takes pleasure in spiritual activity. Spiritual practice brings delight to both the senses and the spirit; each of these two aspects experiences the sweetness according to its own special nature. Spirit, which is the higher part of the soul, is moved more deeply to adore God. Sense, the lower part, wants to wallow in sensual pleasure, grasping for whatever most closely resembles its nature: sensual impurity.

While the spiritual part is with God in profound prayer, the soul may, in spite of herself, be experiencing passive stirrings in her sensual part, which trouble her deeply. These two parts make up the spiritual whole; each will taste of what the other gets, according to its own nature. That is what the philosopher said: Whatever is received comes into the receiver after the manner of that receiver.

Even beginners who have made real progress along the spiritual path may imperfectly receive the spirit of God, since they are still imperfect. But when the soul is purged by the dark night, she no longer suffers these weaknesses. The sensory element is stilled, and the soul receives God purely in her spirit and so everything comes to her in a purely spiritual manner.

When the soul enters a state of prayer or is trying to pray, the Fallen One self may strive to stir up her sensual longings, to disturb and disquiet her. If the soul pays any attention to the imperfections triggered, she will suffer harm. Some beginners grow so afraid of these feelings that they give up on prayer, which is, of course, the very aim of the fragmented self. They have noticed that these attacks occur only in states of prayer. And that's true; the fragmented self assaults the soul at prayer and not during other times precisely to get the soul to quit praying.

Not only that. The Fallen One often vividly conjures impure images and feelings relating to people and things that are actually of great benefit to the soul, just to petrify her. If she gives this anxiety any energy, she will become inclined to avoid considering anything too deeply for fear that she might stumble into trouble.

Those who tend toward depression suffer most in the face of impure thoughts. (Their lives are already so sad; we should have compassion for them!) For those who are afflicted with such bad humor, these trials escalate to unbearable proportions. They are convinced that the Spirit of Evil has direct access to them and that they are powerless against it. Many of these sufferers can, however, through great strength and discipline, ultimately evade the machinations of the Fallen One. Impurities arising from depression are not easily vanquished, however, until the roots of the depression are attacked. (Unless, of course, the dark night flows over the soul and summarily obliterates everything that stands in her way to union with God.)

Impure feelings that wage war upon the soul can be aggravated by her very fear of them. Sometimes the soul will be seeing something or dealing with something or pondering something and all of a sudden she will remember these impurities and grow terrified. This is not her fault.

Some souls are naturally so fragile, so vulnerable, that any spiritual pleasure or profound state of prayer intoxicates them. Their senses are overcome by lust. They find themselves engulfed by the juicy delight of this vice. Passively, the false sweetness endures. Sometimes they are aware that certain acts of impurity and rebellion have taken place inside of them. Their natures are so delicate that the slightest thing stirs them up and heats their blood, giving rise to these impurities. These feelings will also plague them when they are inflamed by anger or burdened by grief or troubled by any other kind of emotional suffering.

Beginners sometimes pay too much attention to whoever is present while they are speaking about spiritual matters or engaged in spiritual practices. They become overcharged by self-importance, slipping into vain satisfaction. This is just another form of spiritual lust. It is accompanied by a general complacency in the will.

Some forge connections with people arising from sensual lust and not from purity of spirit. To test this, they should consciously recall the attraction and see if it causes remembrance and love of God to grow inside them or instead triggers remorse of conscience. If the connection is pure, love for God deepens with the deepening of the friendship. Remembrance of God arises as often as thoughts of the friend arise. Growing inside one love means growing inside the other. The spirit of God is like this. Goodness gives way to the good, because of the harmony between them.

But when this love springs from the vice of lust, it has the contrary effect. As love for the human friend intensifies, love for the divine flows away, even from the memory. The soul who loses herself in that other affection will find her love for God growing cold—remembering one and forgetting the other—which troubles her conscience. On the other hand, as love for God increases in the soul, desire for her human friend may fade away and she can lose her taste for it. This is because the two loves could be contrary. Not only do they fail to feed one another, but the dominant one overwhelms and quenches the fire of the other, enhancing itself, as the philosophers have pointed out.

"That which is born of the flesh is flesh and that which is born of the spirit is spirit," it says in the Gospel. That is, love connected to the senses ends up in sensuality while love that blossoms in the spirit stays with spirit and grows deeper.

# CHAPTER 5

Some of the imperfections of spiritual
anger suffered by beginners.

The unquenched craving many beginners have for spiritual pleasures commonly causes them to suffer from imperfections arising from anger. When the sweet flavors of spiritual states pass, these souls naturally find themselves embittered. And along with the loss of sweetness is a lack of graciousness; any little thing irritates them. Sometimes nobody can stand to be around them.

After the soul has experienced deep absorption in prayer, so pleasing to the sensual part of her nature, she naturally feels vapid and vexed once the condition lifts and the powerful delight passes. She becomes like the child who suffers when the flow of mother's milk is withdrawn. As long as the soul does not indulge in her disappointment, she is not at fault. The distress is simply an imperfection sure to be purified in the intensity of the dark night.

Some souls suffer from another kind of spiritual anger. They watch over others with a kind of restless fervor, perpetually annoyed by the transgressions they perceive. The impulse arises to reprove the other souls in an angry way. Sometimes they even indulge this nasty urge, elevating themselves as masters of virtue. This is all quite contrary to spiritual meekness.

There are others who, when they see their own imperfections, become angry with themselves. This impatience is not humility. They expect to become saints in a day! Many of these beginners have big plans and high intentions, but they are not humble; they fail to question themselves. The more elevated the resolutions they make, the farther their fall and the sharper their anger. They have no patience to wait for God to give them what they need when he sees fit. The remedy for this lack of spiritual meekness is the purification of the dark night.

Of course, there are some souls who God would rather see *less* patient in their progress along the path to him!

———∽∞∿∽———

# CHAPTER 6

*Some of the imperfections of spiritual*
*gluttony suffered by beginners.*

Hardly any beginners, no matter how excellent their progress, avoid falling into some of the myriad imperfections of spiritual gluttony, tempted by the sweet flavors of their initial spiritual experiences. Many, seduced by the delights they discover in spiritual practice, strive more for these tasty juices than for the spiritual purity and wisdom that God is really after throughout the spiritual journey.

In their pursuit of elusive pleasures, their cravings push them to extremes. They transgress the limits of moderation within which virtue resides and develops. Some, lured by the pleasure they find in spiritual practices, kill themselves with penances; others debilitate themselves with fasts, putting far more pressure on themselves than their frail natures can bear.

Are they counseled or commanded to do these things? They are not. In fact, they try to avoid the guides to whom they should be paying closest attention in such matters. They may even dare to do exactly what they have been specifically warned against doing.

These beginners are unreasonable. They forfeit healthy submissiveness, the penance of good sense and discretion, for bodily penance. But mortification of the flesh without surrender is no more than a penance of beasts. Like animals, they are motivated by the peculiar pleasures they find in superficial self-sacrifice. All such extremes are wicked. People who indulge in them are acting from their own personal will, and so they grow in vice and not in virtue. By refusing to walk a path of acquiescence, they get caught in spiritual gluttony and arrogance.

The fragmented self rises up in many beginners, rebelling against wholeness, heightening sensual cravings, stirring gluttony so that they cannot help but try to escape obedience. Submission becomes so distasteful to them they are compelled to modify or rearrange or add to whatever is required of them. For some, this situation gets so bad that any obligation to engage in particular practices makes them lose all devotion and desire to do so. They might as well not even bother to practice at all.

Have you noticed how many of these beginners insist that their spiritual guides give in to their will, trying to manipulate them into conceding? Then, when they do not get what they want, they act like petulant children, walking around in a cloud of gloom. They have this distorted notion that if they are not allowed to do what they want, then they are not serving God, that to please themselves is to satisfy God. They consider their own impulses and gratification to come directly from God! When their guides try to steer them toward the divine will, they grow disheartened and may drop out.

Others, intoxicated by the sweet tidbits they cling to, forget about their own wretchedness and insignificance. They lose touch with their loving dread and awe in the face of God's greatness. They demand that their teachers meet with them all the time. Worse than that, they sometimes dare to engage in sacred rituals without the permission and guidance of those who have earned the privilege to steward souls. They follow their own opinions and conceal the truth. Addicted to self-expression, they express themselves carelessly. So eager to partake of holy rites, they fail to partake with purity and perfection. It would be healthier if they had the opposite inclination and begged their spiritual masters not to call them quite so often to the altar. Between these two extremes, humble resignation is the best. The kind of boldness we speak of is a particularly dangerous thing and will only bring harm.

In ceremonies, beginners may strain to squeeze out feelings of pleasure, instead of offering humble praise and reverence to God within themselves. They are so attached to reaping a sensual harvest that when no such feelings come they think they have failed. This is a negative judgment against God. Don't they realize that the sensory benefits are the least of the gifts offered by the divine? God often withdraws sensual sweetness just so that they might turn the eyes of faith upon him. They desire to feel and taste of God as if he were comprehensible and accessible, not only in group worship but in private spiritual practice, as well. This is an imperfection; it is impurity of faith, in opposition to the divine nature.

These beginners suffer the same kind of imperfection in prayer. They think prayer is all about finding pleasure and sensual devotion. Through great effort, they struggle to acquire that sweetness, exhausting their energy and confounding their heads. When they cannot find what they hunger for, they become discouraged, convinced they have accomplished nothing. In light of this yearning, they lose true devotion and spirituality, which lie in humble and patient perseverance, in self-doubt, in the desire only to serve God.

Such souls give everything over to the pursuit of spiritual gratification and consolation. Beginners like these never get tired of reading sacred literature. They dedicate themselves to one meditation and then another, in constant search of some pleasure in the things of God. Justly and with loving care, God denies them this kind of satisfaction. If indulged, their spiritual gluttony and attachment to that sweetness would lead them into countless troubles. Those who are inclined toward gratification are generally lazy and reluctant to tread the rough road to union. A soul in search of sensory sweetness will naturally turn her face away from the bitterness of self-denial.

Spiritual temperance and forbearance will create a sacred space of sacrifice, awe, and surrender. The soul will begin to see that genuine value does not reside in the multiplicity of spiritual activities or in the delight they bring, but in knowing how to gently deny herself within them.

# CHAPTER 7

*Some of the imperfections of spiritual envy
and laziness suffered by beginners.*

Certain beginners feel disappointed when they perceive the goodness in another. They suffer from profound envy and can hardly bear it when they realize that someone else is ahead of them on the spiritual path. They would rather not hear another be praised. When they find that another's virtues are being celebrated, they can't stand it and are compelled to contradict them. Because no one is saying such great things about them, their annoyance grows; they yearn for preference in all things.

This, of course, is quite contrary to charity, which St. Paul says rejoices in goodness. If there ever is a touch of envy within charity, it is holy envy: a combination of sadness that they do not themselves have the virtues of the other and joy that the other does have them. Mostly, those whose hearts hold charity are happy when another surpasses them in service to God; they are well aware of their own inadequacy in serving him.

Beginners may become bored with the very things that are the most deeply spiritual, which are the things that belie sensory satisfaction. These souls are lazy. They are addicted to sweetness in spiritual practice, impatient when they cannot find it. For their own great good, God may withhold this gratification, to test and prove them. Yet if even one time they reach out in prayer and do not come away with the delights they crave, they may not want to return to it. They may abandon prayer altogether or go about it with serious reluctance.

The way of perfection demands a surrender of personal will and pleasure for the sake of God. Some beginners, trapped by their own laziness, may trade in this perfection for the sweet satisfaction of their own spiritual urges, more interested in following their own will than in trying to discover the will of the divine.

Many find themselves wishing that God would only be aligned with their desires! It makes them sad to have to want what God wants. They have an aversion to adapting their will to God's. They may even have convinced themselves that if something does not please them and correspond with their will, then it must not be God's will, either, and that if they are satisfied, then God must be too. They measure God by themselves and not themselves by God.

This is not in harmony with the teachings of the Gospel which say: "He who loses his will for God shall gain it and he who desires to gain it shall lose it."

Beginners also become irritated when they are directed to do something that holds no pleasure for them. Obsessed by the tasty treats of the spiritual path, they lack the fortitude to engage in the labor demanded by the way of perfection. They resemble those raised in luxury who run away, sad, from everything difficult. The more truly spiritual something is, the more it bores them. Determined to walk the sacred path in accordance with their personal inclinations and the pleasure of their own will, it stirs great pain and resistance in them to embark on that narrow way which is the way of life.

---

This is enough talk about the imperfections suffered in the first stage of the spiritual journey. It is clear how urgent is the need beginners have for God to place them in the state of the adepts. And he does this. He leads them into the dark night. Here is where he weans them from the breasts of personal pleasure, through pure aridity and inner darkness. He removes all the gratuities and childish attachments and helps them acquire the virtues by very different means.

---

May God now give me his divine light so that I may offer something of service in this matter. The night is so dark and the way so difficult to speak of, I need his help.

# CHAPTER 8

*An exploration of the first verse of the first song
and the beginning of an explanation of the "dark night."*

The dark night, which we name "contemplation," creates
two kinds of darkness which align with the two aspects of
human nature: the sensual and the spiritual. In the first
night of purification, the soul is stripped of senses and ac-
commodated to pure spirit. In the other night, the spirit itself is purged and made naked in readiness for the soul's
union of love with God.

The night of sense unfolds for countless beginners. The
night of the spirit is very rare; it comes only to those who are
deeply practiced, deeply disciplined. To the senses, the first
night is bitter and devastating. Yet this does not compare
with the second night, which, as we will see, is horrendous
and terrifying to the spirit. So much has already been writ-
ten about the first night, we will touch on it only briefly now
and move on to explore more profoundly the night of the
spirit, of which hardly anything has been said, either in
speech or in writing. Few souls ever experience it, and those
who do find themselves rendered rightfully speechless.

The style of beginners on the path to God has proven itself to be lowly. Their inclinations have had more to do with pleasing themselves than with loving God. He yearns to carry them forward, now, to pull them up and out of primal desire into a higher form of loving him; to free them of the more basic exercises of sensory discourse with which they have been searching for God with so much trouble and so little success; to lead them into the work of the spirit in which, liberated from basic imperfections, they communicate abundantly with him.

By now, these souls have walked for quite some time along a path of virtue, persevering in meditation and prayer. Through the sweetness and delight they have tasted there, worldly cravings have fallen away. They have gained enough spiritual strength in God to enable them to endure a light burden and a little bit of aridity for him without turning back.

Then, when they are going about their spiritual practices with the greatest enthusiasm and pleasure and it seems to them that the sun of divine favor is shining most brightly upon them, God suddenly darkens all that light. He slams the door shut. He cuts off the source of the spiritual waters they had been drinking from in God as often and as deeply as they desired.

"For, since they were weak and tender, no door was closed unto them," as St. John says in the Apocalypse.

And so he leaves them in such darkness they do not know which way to turn inside their imaginations. With their interior senses engulfed by the night, they cannot advance in discursive meditation as they had always done before. Left in such aridity, not only do they find no satisfaction in their reliable old spiritual practices, but these things actually become tasteless, even bitter.

God sees that these souls have grown a little. He weans them from dependency on the breast so that they can become strong. He lays aside their baby clothes and sets them down from his arms so that they can learn to walk on their own two feet. This feels very strange. Everything seems backwards!

This happens sooner to those beginners who have retreated from the world. Without as much opportunity for backsliding, their appetites turn more quickly and easily away from worldly things. A transformation of desire is essential to enter the blessed night of sense. Once the journey has begun, they do not have to wait long before this night descends.

Being so common, we can find references to the purification of sense everywhere, especially in the Psalms and the Prophets. But I don't want to waste time pointing these out. For those who do not know how to find such scriptures, it does not matter; the prevailing experience of sensory purification speaks for itself.

# CHAPTER 9

*The signs showing that the spiritual seeker is on*
*the path of this night and is immersed in*
*the purification of the senses.*

Internal aridities may not always be the result of the night of sensory purification. Sometimes they arise from transgressions and imperfections, or from laziness and apathy, or from some other kind of bad humor or bodily weakness.

One of the signs that this dryness indicates the passage into purification is that while the soul finds no pleasure in the things of God, she does not find consolation in any created thing either. Since God has placed the soul in this dark night to dry up and purify her sensual thirst, he no longer allows her to taste sweetness or delight in anything whatsoever. You can tell that such aridity and bitterness is probably not the outcome of some recently committed transgression or imperfection because if it were, the sensory part of the soul would be drawn to indulge in something besides divine things. Whenever the appetite relaxes into some imperfection, the soul immediately feels inclined toward that thing, either a little or a lot, depending on how attached she has grown to it.

Another indication of true purification is that the memory is carried constantly back to God with a depth of caring that is actually painful to the soul. She thinks that she must not be serving God, that she is backsliding, because there is no sweetness left for her in divine things. It is clear that this kind of aversion is not the fruit of laziness or apathy. If it were, the soul would not care so deeply about whether or not she is being of service to God. There is a significant difference between spiritual aridity and general apathy. Apathy is informed by laziness, a weakness of spiritual will, devoid of any concern about serving God. But purifying dryness holds within itself a longing, a passionate concern, and grief about not serving God.

Even though this aridity might be intensified by accompanying depression, it does not fail to have a purifying effect on the appetite. The soul is stripped of the distraction of all pleasures and her attention is centered on God alone. If it were merely a matter of foul humor, it would lead to nothing but disgust and the ruin of the soul's very nature. She would not be burning with the desire to serve God that accompanies true purifying dryness. At the same time that this purgative aridity evaporates all sweet juices, causing the sensory part of the soul to turn feeble and come crashing down, the spirit has quietly grown ready and strong.

God has transferred goodness and power from the senses to the spirit. Unable to make use of these precious gifts, the senses are left fallow, desiccated, void. While the spirit is feasting, the sensory part of the soul is starving; it grows too weak to act. But the spirit thrives on this banquet, growing stronger and more alert, her yearning to be true to God more profound than ever.

At first, focused as she is on the absence of familiar sweetness, the soul may not notice the spiritual delight. This is because the exchange is still strange to her. Her tastes are accustomed to those old sensory pleasures, and she remains on the lookout for them. The spiritual palate has not yet been purified and attuned to such subtle delight. She will not appreciate the fruits of this spiritual bounty but will only suffer thirst and famine until she is groomed for it through the dry, dark night. The pleasures she once harvested so abundantly that she had come to expect them now evade her.

Those whom God begins to lead into the solitude of the desert are like the children of Israel. God gave them manna from heaven to eat, which contained within itself all flavors and turned into the taste each of them most hungered for. Still, all they could feel was their craving for the meats and onions they ate in Egypt. This is what they were used to, and this is what they preferred over the delicate sweetness of the angelic manna. In the midst of that divine food, they wept and sighed for flesh. Our appetite can be so base that it makes us long for our own wretched rations, repulsed by incomparable heavenly plentitude.

But when dry stretches appear along the path of the purification of sensual desire, the soul finds herself drawing strength and energy to do her work from the substance of this interior food, even though she might not at first experience its full flavor. This is the beginning of true contemplation. It is dark and empty to the senses, a secret contemplation, hidden even from the one who is experiencing it. This contemplation usually kindles an inclination and a yearning to be alone and in quietude. The soul will not be able to conceptualize a single thing, nor have any desire to do so.

If only souls that this happens to could just be quiet, setting aside all concern about accomplishing any task—interior or exterior—and quit troubling themselves about doing anything! Soon, within that very stillness and release, they would begin to taste subtly of that interior nourishment, a nourishment so delicate that if they were purposely to try they could never taste it. This work only happens when the soul is at ease and free from care. It's like the air which eludes the hand that tries to grasp it. "Turn your eyes away from me, because they are making me fly away," says the lover to the Beloved in The Song of Songs. God leads the soul into this state by such a singular manner that if she tries to employ her old faculties, she will not contribute one bit to the work of God but in fact hinder it.

In contemplation, when the soul leaves behind the functions of the discursive mind and enters the state of the adept, it is God who is working in her. He binds up her interior faculties, withdrawing support from the intellect, squeezing the juice out of the will and leaving nothing in the memory. Whatever the soul tries to do of her own accord during this time is of no use but serves only as an obstacle to inner peace. This peace—so delicate and subtle—does its work in stillness and in solitude. It is far removed from all those earlier spiritual delights, which were palpable and sensual. This is the peace that, says David, God speaks in the soul to make of her that which is purely spiritual.

Another sign that the soul is being blessed by this purification of the senses is that no matter how hard she tries, she finds herself powerless to intellectualize or to feel the flow of imagination like she used to. God no longer communicates himself through the senses. He does not make himself known through the analytical mind, which synthesizes and divides ideas. Instead, he begins to come through pure spirit, through simple contemplation, untainted by discursive thought. Neither the exterior nor the interior senses, which belong to the lower part of the soul, can touch her in this place. From here on, imagination cannot find protection. Fantasy conjures no foothold.

This discomfort and dissatisfaction has nothing to do with bad humor. If that's all it were, then the mood would pass, as such things do, and the soul, with a little effort, would again find support for the faculties of sense and reason. But when the soul enters true purification of desire, she becomes increasingly unable to engage her faculties.

Some souls in the beginning will not suffer from continuous deprivation of sensual pleasure and cognitive ability. Because of their fragility, it may not be possible to wean them with a single blow to the senses. Yet, if they are to move along on their journey, they will enter ever more deeply into that wilderness where the mechanisms of the sensory self cease to function.

It is different for souls not bound for union. They do not have to endure perpetual aridity of the senses. Sometimes they feel empty, sometimes filled. At times they can formulate concepts, other times they cannot. God places them in this night just to temper them, to humble them, to cleanse their appetites and curb their craving for spiritual sweetness. These are not the souls who he leads into contemplation, which is the path of the spirit. Not even half of those who commit themselves to a spiritual life are led by God into this contemplation. God best knows why. For this reason, he never weans their senses permanently from the breasts of discursive meditation, but only for small moments, in certain seasons of their lives.

# CHAPTER 10

*The way the soul must conduct herself
in this dark night.*

The deep suffering of the soul in the night of sense comes not so much from the aridity she must endure but from this growing suspicion that she has lost her way. She thinks that all spiritual blessing is over and that God has abandoned her. She finds neither support nor delight in holy things. Growing weary, she struggles in vain to practice the tricks that used to yield results, applying her faculties to some object of meditation in hopes of finding satisfaction. She thinks that if she is making a conscious effort to do this and still feels nothing, then she must be accomplishing nothing. Nevertheless, she perseveres, plagued by reluctance and fatigue. In truth, though unaware, the soul has been basking in spaciousness and quietude, free from the manipulations of her faculties.

And so the soul finds herself rejecting the things of God and yet harvesting no benefit on her own. In searching for spirit, she actually loses the spirit of peace and tranquility in which she has been spontaneously dwelling. She is like someone who abandons what he has been doing in order to turn around and do it all over again, or someone who leaves the city only to come right back and reenter it, or someone who releases his prey so that he can hunt it once more. The soul's efforts are fruitless.

If there is nobody to understand her, she is at risk of giving up and abandoning the path at this juncture, or at least of obstructing her own progress. Persistent in pursuing the way of mental prayer, she exhausts her very nature, then thinks she is failing as a result of her own negligence and sinfulness. But this diligence is vacuous! God is now leading her down another path, far different from the first. One is a path of the mind, but true contemplation transcends discursive thought and imagination.

(Those of you who find yourselves in this predicament need to comfort yourselves. Patiently persevere and do not let yourselves get upset. Trust in God, who does not abandon those who seek him with a simple and righteous heart. He will not neglect to give you what you need for your path until he delivers you into that clear, pure light of love. You are meant to receive this great gift, yet it is only through the dark night of the spirit that he will bring you to it.)

This is no time for discursive meditation. Instead, the soul must surrender into peace and quietude, even if she is convinced she is doing nothing and wasting time. She might assume that this lack of desire to think about anything is a sure sign of her laziness. But simple patience and perseverance in a state of formless prayerfulness, while doing nothing, accomplishes great things.

All that is required here is to set her soul free, unencumbered, to let her take a break from ideas and knowledge, to quit troubling herself about thinking and meditating. The soul must content herself with a loving attentiveness toward God, without agitation, without effort, without the desire to taste or feel him. These urges only disquiet and distract the soul from the peaceful quietude and sweet ease inherent in the gift of contemplation being offered.

The soul might continue to have qualms about wasting time. She may wonder if it would not be better to be doing something else, since she cannot think or activate anything in prayer. Let her bear these doubts calmly. There is no other way to go to prayer now than to surrender to this sweet ease and breadth of spirit. If the soul tries to engage her interior faculties to accomplish something, she will squander the goodness God is instilling in her through the peace in which she is simply resting.

It would be as if a painter were composing a portrait and the model kept shifting because she felt like she had to be doing something! She would be disturbing the master's work, preventing him from accomplishing his masterpiece. What the soul really wants is to abide in inner peace and ease. Any activity, preference, or notion she might feel inclined toward will only distract her, intensifying her awareness of sensory emptiness. The harder the soul struggles to find support through knowledge and affection, the more she will feel their lack.

The best thing for the soul to do is to pay no attention to the fact that the actions of her faculties are slipping away. Instead, she should desire that this happen swiftly! She needs to get out of the way. In peaceful plenitude, let her now say "yes" to the infused contemplation God is bestowing upon her. This makes space in the spirit for enkindling, the burning of that dark and secret love that contemplation brings with it and presses into the soul. Contemplation is nothing other than a secret, peaceful, loving inflow of God. If given room, it will fire the soul in the spirit of love, which is just what she declares in the next line:

*"Inflamed by love-longing . . ."*

# CHAPTER 11

*Explores the first lines of the first verse.*

In the beginning, the soul might not feel the flame of love. Either her nature is still impure and has not yet caught fire, or else she has not cultivated a peaceful place inside herself. And yet, at times, she will begin to feel a certain yearning for God. The more this intensifies, the closer the soul is drawn to God, beginning to burn brightly in love for him. She does not know or understand where such love and longing come from.

Sometimes this flame, this sweet blazing, grows so intense that the soul's love-longing for God is like David's who, in his own dark night, cried out: "Because my heart was inflamed (in contemplative love), my reins, too, were changed." His desire was changed from the way of sense to the way of spirit. "And," he says, "I was dissolved into nothing and annihilated and I knew nothing."

Having no idea where she is heading, the soul watches herself being annihilated by all the things of above and below that once brought such pleasure. She finds herself madly in love, without knowing why. At times, the fire of love burns so hot in the spirit and the soul's longing mounts to such a passion that she feels as if her very bones were drying up in this thirst. Her nature seems to be shriveling, her natural powers fading, their warmth and strength wiped out by the magnitude of this thirsty love. This thirst is a living thing. "My soul thirsts for the living God," says David, as though this thirst were alive. We could even say, "This thirst is killing me!" Although there will always be some thirst along the way, its intensity is mercifully occasional, not constant.

At first, the soul feels sheer aridity and emptiness. Love is enkindled later. In the midst of the barrenness of the natural faculties arises a prevailing concern and solicitude toward God, accompanied by grief and dread that she is not serving him. (Such a distressed spirit, whose sole intent is soliciting God's love, is a sacrifice that pleases him more than a little.) Once the aridities have, to some degree, purified the sensual nature of its ordinary compulsions, this mindfulness and caring lead the soul into secret contemplation. Only then can divine love be ignited in the spirit.

Meanwhile, however, like a person who is in the process of being cured of some ailment, the soul experiences only suffering within the dark, dry purification of her natural appetite. She is being healed of imperfections and growing in virtue. Soon, she will be equal to meeting that great love, as we see in the next line:

*"O exquisite risk!"*

The soul is gaining so many benefits that she considers it to be nothing less than a "joyous risk" to, through the pure grace of this dark night, make her escape from the fetters of sense that have bound her lower nature. All the advantages discovered in this night, which turn the passage through darkness into a matter of immeasurably good fortune, are reflected in the next line:

*"Undetected I slipped away."*

The soul responds to the quelling of sensual activity by going forth from herself. Remember when she used to seek God through those feeble, limited, and ineffectual manipulations? At every step she stumbled into a thousand ignorances and imperfections! Once the night quenches all sensory satisfaction in the soul, whether of above or below, and darkens the discursive mind, it liberates her, bestowing innumerable blessings. The soul grows vastly in virtue. It will be a thing of great consolation to the seeker who treads such a rough road to discover that what seemed so severe and adverse to spiritual gratification yields such an abundance of blessings.

Now the soul, inspired by the night, moves beyond created things and journeys toward eternal things. This is cause for celebration! What a boon for the soul to have her attachments severed at last! How many souls are ever able to endure this? How many persevere in passing through the tiny gate and walking the narrow path that leads to Life? Hardly any. The small gate is the night of sense. To pass through, the soul must be stripped and laid bare. She has to ground herself in pure faith, completely contrary to all things sensual. Only then can she go forth on that narrow path, which is the night of spirit. Through pure faith, the soul travels to God and becomes one with him.

CHAPTER 12

*The benefits this night brings to the soul.*

Just as Abraham made a great feast when his son Isaac was weaned, so there is rejoicing in heaven when God removes the baby clothes from the soul. He is setting her down from his arms and making her walk on her own two feet. He removes her lips from the milky breast and replaces the soft, sweet mush of infants with the crusty bread of the robust.

The most essential benefit of infused contemplation is self-knowledge. The soul becomes acutely aware of her own insignificance. The countless mercies God bestows upon the soul now come wrapped in this self-knowledge, informed by the aridity and emptiness of the faculties. In light of the abundance previously enjoyed and the difficulty now encountered in spiritual labor, the soul cannot help but notice her own wretchedness, which was invisible in her time of prosperity.

In the Book of Exodus, God wishes to humble the children of Israel and make them know themselves, so he commands them to strip off the fancy garments in which they had been roaming the desert, saying: "From now on, leave aside your festive ornaments and put on common working clothes, that you might know the treatment you merit." In other words, when you wear clothing appropriate to celebration and mirth, you feel less humble than you should. Take off this attire. Clothe yourself in humility, that you may know who you really are and what is rightfully yours.

The time when the soul went around all dressed up for a party was a time when she was finding plenty of gratification and support from God in spiritual practice. She was happy and satisfied then, convinced that she was, in some way, serving him. Now, dressed in the working clothes of aridity and desolation, all her earlier lights darkened, the soul shines more clearly in the virtue of self-knowledge. She experiences herself to be nothing, now. She finds absolutely no satisfaction in self. She knows that on her own she neither does nor can do anything.

God cherishes the soul's absence of self-satisfaction and her sorrow in not serving him. This means far more than any of the spiritual pleasures in which she used to indulge, and more than any of her religious doings; no matter how lofty they may have been, these deeds were the occasion of many imperfections and unconsciousness. Innumerable blessings flow from the fountain that is the source of self-knowledge to the soul that is humbly clothed in the cloak of aridity.

The soul is learning to commune with God more respectfully, now, and more courteously. This is the way one should always approach the Most High. In the prosperity of gratification and consolation, the soul had forgotten how to be. The sweet flavors she had been tasting heightened her craving for him and made her more daring than was appropriate, more discourteous and inconsiderate.

When Moses perceived that God was speaking to him, he was so blinded by elation that he would have gone to him without hesitation if God had not commanded him to stay still and take off his shoes. To commune with God, nakedness of desire must be coupled with respect and discretion. When Moses had acquiesced to God's command, he became so discrete and careful that he not only did not dare to come near to God, but he dared not even reflect on him. Having removed the shoes of his appetite, he became fully conscious of his own insignificance before God. This is fitting for a soul on the verge of apprehending the word of God.

God did not prepare Job to speak with him by indulging his delights and glories. That was how Job used to experience connection with his God. No, God stripped Job naked and left him on a dunghill, vulnerable and persecuted by his friends. The ground was teeming with worms. Job was filled with anguish and bitterness. This is exactly when God Most High, he who lifts the poor man from the dunghill, was pleased to come down and speak with him face-to-face. This is when God revealed to Job the depths and heights of his wisdom, which he had never done in the time of Job's prosperity.

Here is another blessing yielded by the dark night of

sense: God illumines the soul. He does this by supplementing her knowledge of her own insignificance with awareness of the greatness and excellence of God. The Prophet Isaiah says: "Your light shall shine in the darkness." God cleanses the soul of attachment to sensory content, leaving the understanding limpid and free so that it can grasp truth.

Sensory pleasure and desire, even in spiritual experience, obscures and obstructs the spirit. A state of predicament quickens and illumines the understanding. Vexation makes us see how, through the blessing of this dark, dry night of contemplation, God supernaturally imparts his divine wisdom to an empty and unburdened soul. God did not share this inflow along with those first sweet juices because the soul was too crowded.

The Prophet Isaiah asks: "To whom shall God teach his knowledge? And whom shall he make to understand his message?" To those, he answers, who are drawn away from the breasts and weaned from their milk. The first milk of spiritual sweetness fosters attachment to the succulent breasts of mental prayer. This is the realm of the senses. It cannot prepare the soul for the direct inflow of the divine.

To hear God, one must stand strong, detached from sensory affection. "I will stand upon my watch," says the Prophet (that is, detachment from desire), "and make firm my step (that is, not meditate with the faculty of sense) in order to dwell in contemplation (that is, in order to apprehend what may come to me from God)."

And so from this dry night first flows self-knowledge and

from this source arises knowledge of God. St. Augustine cries out: "Let me know myself, Lord, that I may know thee!" As the philosophers say, one extreme is well known by another.

David says: "In the desert, without water, dry and without a path, I appeared before you that I might behold your power and glory." The teaching offered here is a beautiful thing. It is not the spiritual delights and satisfactions David experienced that prepared him for knowing God but rather the aridities and detachment of the senses, which is what is meant here by the dry and desert land. He says, too, that the way which led to his experience of the glory of God was not through divine concepts and meditations, which he had so often used before. David encountered God in the midst of his utter inability to conjure up any notion of God. He could not walk with the aid of the discursive mind or the imagination; this is the land with no path.

What the soul draws also from the aridity and emptiness of the night of desire is spiritual humility. Through humility, acquired along with self-knowledge, the soul is purified of the imperfections of spiritual pride into which she stumbled during her time of prosperity. Aware only of her own aridity and misery, it never occurs to her that she is now making better progress than others, which is what she used to erroneously believe. Now she is sure that others are doing much better than she is. From this humility arises love of neighbor. The soul honors others and does not judge them as she did before, when she assumed that she burned with special fervor and that they did not. Her own wretchedness is so present in her sight that there is no room to scrutinize others.

"I fell mute, humbled," says David. "I kept silence in blessing and my sorrow was renewed." It seemed to him that all that was good in his soul had been entirely depleted. Not only could he find no speech to express it, but the grief he suffered about his own insignificance left him mute concerning his neighbor.

These souls are growing submissive and yielding on the spiritual path. When they recognize how miserable they are, they begin listening closely to the teachings of others and opening themselves to anyone who might be able to guide them and tell them what to do. The presumption that overcame them in their prosperity disappears. The imperfections of spiritual pride are swept away.

# CHAPTER 13

*Other benefits this night of sense
brings to the soul.*

As the night deepens, God continues to restrain sensual desire, pressing into the soul, healing and humbling her. The soul loses the power of her sensory passions. Receiving no satisfaction, the senses become sterile. The appetite loses all its juice, just as udders will dry up when no longer pumped for the flow of milk. Once sensual desire is quelled, the soul dwells in spiritual peace and equanimity. Where there is no sensual hunger, there is no disturbance, but only serenity and solace.

From this arises another benefit: continual remembrance of God. This is coupled with a dread of moving backwards on the spiritual path. Among the advantages of this purification of the senses, this is one of the greatest. The soul is washed clean of the imperfections which had been clinging to her on the wings of appetite and craving, leaving her darkened and dull.

Here is another boon granted to the soul in this night: all the virtues come together in harmony. In response to emptiness and aridity, the soul practices the virtues of patience and long suffering, persevering in spiritual practices without gratification. She exercises the virtue of holy charity when, no longer motivated by the tasty delights she finds in practice, she is moved only by God. She manifests the virtue of fortitude because the difficulties and troubles she finds in her spiritual work cause her to draw strength from weakness.

And so from this night the soul harvests four great gifts: the delight of peace; continuous remembrance of God and caring for him; clarity and purity of soul; and the practice of virtue. "My soul refused consolations, I remembered God and found consolation, I exercised myself and my soul swooned away," says David. "I meditated with my heart at night and exercised myself and I swept and purified my spirit."

The soul is also purged of the spiritual imperfections of wrath, envy, and sloth; she acquires the virtues that balance them out. She is softened and humbled by the hardships God offers in the course of the dark night. In this way, she grows meek toward God, toward herself, and toward her neighbor. She no longer gets angry with herself over her own faults, harsh with her neighbor over his, or disturbed with God that he has not made her instantly perfect.

Now the soul has cultivated generosity toward others. If she has any envy, it will not be vicious like it was when it gave her such pain to see others preferred and more advanced along the path. Her grief comes only from seeing her own wretchedness. Any envy she suffers is in itself holy, since all she wants is to be like the others, which is itself a great virtue.

The sloth and tedium the soul suffers in spiritual practice are no longer imperfections. These impurities used to arise in response to the sensory satisfaction she experienced in spiritual states or which she mourned when such pleasure was not forthcoming. But this new weariness does not come from sensual weakness, since God has already purified the soul of her appetites by eliminating sensual gratification.

Innumerable benefits flow into the soul that sits in dry contemplation. In the midst of hardship, when least expected, God will often transmit to the soul the purest sweetness and love, and an unutterably delicate spiritual awareness. These gifts are immeasurably greater than all the others the soul previously clung to. It's just that, in the beginning, she won't think so, since the spiritual inflow is so rarefied it is invisible to the senses.

The soul walks her path now with purity in love of God. Not moved to act from the satisfaction derived of her own spiritual deeds, all she cares about is God. She is not presumptuous. She is not self-satisfied. She is timid and distrustful of herself, without a trace of self-importance. Holy awe sustains and deepens the virtues. A profound yearning to serve God grows inside the soul. As the breasts of sensuality dry up, they no longer sustain the desires the soul once pursued. Her longing is highly pleasing to God since, as David says: "The suffering spirit is a sacrifice to God."

# CHAPTER 14

*Explains the last line of the first song.*

When the house of sense was stilled, when, through this blessed night of purification her passions were quenched, when her desires had been laid to rest and fallen asleep, the soul could slip away at last and begin her journey along the spiritual path. This is the road of the adept, which by another name is called the Illuminative Way, or the Way of Infused Contemplation. Now God himself feeds and refreshes the soul without the active participation of her discursive mind.

Remember: only a few souls ever pass beyond the night of sensory purification and into the more formidable night of the spirit where divine union unfolds. This first night is accompanied by potent trials and sensual temptations, which last for a long time—longer for some souls than for others.

Some are visited by the Fallen One in the form of lust, whose mission is to assault the senses with powerful, unspeakable temptations and to arouse the spirit with seductive notions and vivid images that burn in the imagination. This can be a pain worse than death to the soul.

At other times, a spirit of chilling irreverence creeps into the night. It roams among all the soul's thoughts and ideas, introducing unbearable sacrilege. Sometimes profanities rise up in the imagination with such force that the soul almost finds herself giving voice to them, which is excruciating.

At times, another dreadful spirit which Isaiah calls *Spiritus vertiginis* comes to the soul, not to knock her down but to try her. This spirit so darkens the senses that they become filled with a thousand qualms and perplexities, so intricate that the soul's judgment can never be satisfied, and she cannot find support in any counsel or concept. This is one of the most horrific challenges of the night and is very similar to what is to come in the night of the spirit.

God usually sends these storms and trials in the night of sensory purification to those whom he will put into that other night afterwards. Chastened and buffeted, the senses and the faculties are honed, made ready for union with wisdom, which will be given there. After all, if, through trials and temptations, a soul is not tempted and tried, if she is not tested and proved, how can her senses be quickened with wisdom? In Ecclesiasticus we are asked: "He who is not tempted, what does he know? And he who is not proved, what are the things he realizes?" Jeremiah says: "You have chastised me, Lord, and I have been given teaching."

We cannot know for certain how long the soul will be

held in this fasting and penance of the senses. Not everyone goes through the same thing or faces identical temptations. Everything is given in accordance with the will of God, in proportion to the greater or lesser degree of imperfection each soul needs to purge away. God humbles a soul with more or less intensity and for a longer or shorter period of time to match the level of union in love to which he wishes to raise her.

Those who have greater strength and capacity for suffering God purifies more intensively and more quickly. But the weak ones he keeps for a very long time in this first night, purging them gently, tempting them lightly. He frequently refreshes their senses so that they will not give up. These souls come to the purity of perfection late in life, if at all. They are never fully in this night nor fully outside of it. Even though they make no real progress, God exercises them once in a while with temptations and aridities to cultivate humility and self-knowledge. In some seasons, he answers their call for help with divine solace so they will not lose courage and go back to their search for worldly consolation. God himself walks with weaker souls, now appearing, now disappearing, exercising them in his love. Without the turnings away, they would never learn to reach for him.

# BOOK II

---◅◦◦◦▻---

# NIGHT

*of the*

# SPIRIT

# CHAPTER 1

*Explores the dark night of spiritual purification.*

What joy! The soul has emerged victorious from the tribulations of the night of sensory purification. She has risen above the state of the beginner and entered the state of the adept. God may not immediately move her into the night of the spirit, now. Instead, the soul may spend years cultivating mastery before she is ready to face the impenetrable darkness that leads to union.

In this phase, the soul is like someone who has escaped from prison. She goes about the things of God with freedom and satisfaction. Now that the faculties are no longer attached to the discursive mind or troubled by the spiritual anxiety that used to bind the soul, her interior delight flows more abundantly than it ever did before she entered that first dark night. Without the labor of the intellect, she now finds within her the most serene and loving contemplation and spiritual sweetness.

But the purification of the soul is not over. The essential part is still to come, which is spiritual purification. Sense and spirit belong to one whole: the soul; there is an inherent connection between them. No matter how profound the purgation of sense may have been, the purification of the soul is not complete until the spirit, too, is purged. And so the soul still suffers certain aridities, darknesses, and dangers. These can be much more intense than the perils of the past. They are omens which herald the coming of the night of spirit. But they do not last, as they will in the night to come. After having spent a while in this stormy darkness, the soul soon returns to her customary serenity.

This is how God purifies souls not meant to ascend to such an elevated degree of love as those who will ultimately merge with him. He brings them into the night of spirit at intervals, causing night to descend and then dawn to spread its wings over them. David says: "He sends his crystal (contemplation) like morsels." These morsels of contemplation are never as intense as that awesome and irrevocable contemplative night that leads to divine union.

God communicates sweetness and interior delight to these adept souls more abundantly, now. It overflows into their senses with much greater ease than before the sensory purification. Now that the senses are cleansed, they can more readily access the pleasures of the spirit.

But the sensory component of the soul is, by its very nature, feeble. It will never be able to meet the powerful thrustings of the spirit. And so, these fragile adepts, in response to communications from the spiritual part of the soul, suffer wounds and queasiness. This fatigues the spirit. As the Wise

Man says: "The corruptible body presses down the soul" (Wis. 9:15). As a result, the communications cannot be too strong or too spiritual, even though intensity is required to catalyze divine union with God. The senses which have to share them are just too weak and imperfect to take it.

Raptures and transports happen when communion is not purely spiritual. Once divine blessings are imparted straight to the spirit, as they will be to the perfected ones already purified by the second spiritual night, the enchantments and torments of the body cease. The soul enjoys liberation of spirit. Her senses are no longer clouded and carried away.

# CHAPTER 2

*Other imperfections of these adepts.*

Some imperfect habits and affections have remained in the soul like roots; the purification of sense has not penetrated them. They are as difficult to remove as a stain that is old and ingrained in comparison to a fresh spill.

Remember: the purification of sense is only the gateway to infused contemplation, which leads to the purification of the spirit. It serves more to integrate sense with spirit than to unite the spirit with God. The stains of the old being remain in the spirit, though they may not be visible. If they are not wiped clean by the soap and strong lye of this second night of purgation, the spirit cannot come into the purity of divine love.

These souls may also suffer from the natural deadening of the mind everyone contracts through wickedness. Their spirit is distracted by external things. They must be illumined, clarified, and brought back to remembrance by the challenges and perils of the night. These habitual imperfections, which souls which have not passed beyond the state of adepts find within themselves, cannot coexist with the perfection of union in love.

Of course, not everyone falls into imperfection in the same way. Some, whose spiritual goodness is especially superficial and connected to the senses, slip into graver difficulties and dangers. They find their hands overfull of spiritual communications and perceptions arising in both the senses and the spirit. They often behold imaginary spiritual visions. The Spirit of Evil plays tricks on them, delighting in suggesting dramatic impressions and feelings. Unless the soul is careful to defend herself strongly against these kinds of chimeras and to surrender ever more fully in her faith, she will be easily beguiled and deluded.

This is where the Spirit of Evil makes many souls believe in vain visions and false prophesies. This is where they may conclude that God and the saints are talking to them. This is where they are filled with presumption and pride. Moved by vanity and arrogance, they allow themselves to be caught up in external displays that make them appear holy, like trances and other exhibitions. They become bold with God. They lose holy awe, which is the key and the gatekeeper of all the other virtues.

So many illusions and deceptions multiply in some of these souls and so ingrained do they become that it becomes doubtful these souls will ever return to the pure path of simple virtue and true spirituality. They collapse into misery because they have given themselves over too easily to these spiritual phenomena. And just when they were starting to make some real progress along the path!

These imperfections are less curable than the earlier ones simply because they think these blessings are more spiritual than the others. I could go on and on about the dangers at this juncture, but I will restrain myself. I will say only this, and only to establish how necessary it is for the soul who would move forward on her path to enter the purification which is the night of spirit: that no adept, no matter how strenuous her efforts, will ever be able to avoid all of these natural affections and imperfect habits. These must be purified by God before the soul may pass into divine union with him.

Besides, if the lower part of the soul still shares in these spiritual communications, they cannot be as pure and powerful as they need to be for the soul to reach union. To come to union, the soul must fully enter the second night of spirit. This is where both sense and spirit are stripped of all perceptions and flavors. The soul is made to walk in darkness and pure faith. As Hosea says: "I will betroth thee (that is, I will unite you) with me through faith."

# CHAPTER 3

*A glimpse of what is to come.*

The soul has spent significant time feeding the senses with sweet communications from the Beloved. Allured by spiritual delights, savoring the flavors that have flowed from the spirit into the senses, the sensory element of the soul can now be melded with the spirit. Both aspects of the soul can now partake of the same spiritual feast from the same platter, as one being with a single purpose. Together, they are ready to suffer the arduous purification of the spirit that awaits them.

This is when both the sensory and the spiritual aspects of the soul will become thoroughly purified. Since one part of the soul can never be wholly purged without the other, the true purification of the senses begins with the purification of the spirit. All the imperfections of the sensory element are rooted in the spirit and draw their strength from there. This is where the senses cultivate all their habits, good and bad. Until these are purged, the soul will not be fully purified of the wicked uprisings of sense.

It's a good thing that the soul has passed through the storms of the first night and has gotten to spend some time breathing in the fair weather that followed. Now sense, commingled with spirit, can endure purification with greater fortitude. Unless the soul is first healed of sensual weakness and then fortified by the sweet and delicious communion she tastes in God, her nature will lack the strength and readiness to bear it.

These proficient souls still deal with God in a somewhat lowly and instinctual way. The gold of the spirit is not yet purified and illumined. They "think of God as little children and speak of God as little children and feel and experience God as little children," as St. Paul says. They have not reached the state of perfection which is union of the soul with God. Fully grown, they will accomplish mighty works in the spirit through this union, their deeds and powers more divine than human.

God strips them of the old being and clothes them in the new, which, says the Apostle, "God has created in the very newness of sense." He denudes the faculties, the affections, and the senses—spiritual and sensual, inner and outer. He leaves the understanding dark, the will dried up, the memory vacuous, and the affections tormented by bitterness and anguish. He takes away from the soul the feelings of pleasure she used to enjoy from spiritual blessings. This deprivation is one of the principal requirements for the union of love.

# CHAPTER 4

*Explores the first song of the soul again, this time
in light of the purification of the spirit.*

> *On a dark night,*
> *Inflamed by love-longing—*
> *O exquisite risk!—*
> *Undetected I slipped away.*
> *My house, at last, grown still.*

The soul is saying something like this:

I am blessedly poverty-stricken. Without support from any of the perceptions of my soul, in the void of my intellect and the captivity of my will, in the desolation and anguish of my memory, left in the darkness of my faith, my will alone touched by the grief and tribulation of my love-longings for God, I went out of myself. I transcended the limits of my own understanding, my feeble way of loving, and my impoverished and limited form of appreciating God. Neither sensuality nor the Fallen One could block my way. This was a great blessing and an exquisite risk for me. With the faculties, passions, and desires of my soul stilled and annihilated,

I moved from my own human dealings and activities into the dealings and activities of God. My understanding departed from itself. It changed from natural to divine.

When the soul connects with God through this purification, she no longer acquires knowledge by means of her natural energy and light; instead, she knows through the divine wisdom with which she has been unified.

And my will, too, the soul is saying, departed from itself. It became divine. United now with divine love, it no longer loves with its natural powers in an inferior way. It loves with the purity and potency of the divine. Near to God, my will cannot act in its old human manner. My memory too has been transfigured in glimpses of eternal glory.

See how the dark night revivifies the powers and inclinations of the soul with divine courage and delight!

Let's look at that first line, again:

*"On a dark night . . ."*

# CHAPTER 5

*Revisits the first line and begins to explain how
dark contemplation is not only night for
the soul but also grief and torment.*

The dark night of the spirit is an inflowing of God into the soul. It purges her of imperfections: natural and spiritual. Contemplatives call it "infused contemplation" or "mystical theology." This is where God transmits his secret teachings to the soul and instructs her in the perfection of love. She does not have to do a thing, nor will she understand a thing. Infused contemplation is the wisdom of the loving God. It both purges and illumines the soul, making her ready for the union of love. The same loving wisdom that purifies and en-lightens the blessed spirits on other planes of existence, purges and illumines the earthly soul, now.

But here is the doubt: Why is this divine light, which il-lumines and purges the soul of ignorance, called here the "dark night"?

Divine wisdom is not only night and darkness to the soul but also terror and suffering. Its height transcends the natu-ral reach of the soul and so it looks like darkness to her. Her own insignificance and impurity also cause her to experience the light of God as painful and oppressive. The Philosopher suggests that the clearer and more manifest are divine things in themselves, the darker and more hidden they are to the natural eyes of the soul. The brighter the light, the more blinding it is to the owl. The more directly we gaze at the sun, the more it darkens our visual faculty, depriving it and overwhelming it, because of its inherent weakness.

And so, when divine light strikes the soul that is not yet fully illumined, it causes spiritual darkness to drop over her, transcending her limitations, impoverishing and darkening her natural intelligence. St. Dionysus and other mystics call infused contemplation a "ray of darkness." The power of the discursive mind is conquered by this great supernatural light.

David says that "near to God and surrounding him are darkness and clouds." It's not that this is actually so but that it seems that way to the feeble intellect which is blinded by such radiance and cannot rise to meet it. "Through the great splendor of his presence," says David, "clouds passed," that is, between God and our own understanding. When God sends forth from himself the illuminating ray of secret wisdom to the soul not yet fully transformed, her mind is enveloped by darkness.

Divine infused contemplation is an exceedingly excellent thing; the soul that receives this gift and has not been wholly purified is filled with misery, which is an exceedingly bad thing. Because these two contraries cannot coexist in a single subject, the soul will undergo pain and suffering. The soul becomes a battlefield where these two contraries wage war against one another.

The light and wisdom of this contemplation are so pure and bright and the soul it invades is so dark and impure that their meeting is going to be painful. When the eyes are bad—impure and sickly—clear light feels like an ambush and it hurts. Because of her impurity, the soul suffers deeply when she is directly assaulted by this divine light. When the pure light charges the fortress of the soul with the purpose of dispelling her impurity, she feels so tainted and wretched that it seems God must have turned against her and that she must have set herself against God, as well. Her pain is so deeply felt because she strongly suspects that God has given up on her. "Why have you set me against you and made of me such a heavy burden to myself?" Job demands of God.

Illumined by this pure light and yet plunged into darkness, the soul clearly perceives her own impurity. She is sure that she is unworthy of God and of any creature. What distresses her most is the certainty that she never will be worthy, and that all blessings have ended for her. The mind is profoundly immersed in the knowledge and feeling of its limitations and miseries. The divine and dark light reveals to the eye of the soul the truth that, of her own power, she will never be any other way. David says: "For his iniquity you have corrected man and have undone and consumed his soul, as the arts of the spider are unraveled."

The soul is naturally, morally, and spiritually so fragile that divine wisdom assails her with considerable force. While this ultimately strengthens and soothes her, she suffers so much in her weakness that she nearly swoons away. This is especially true during those times when the soul is struck most powerfully, when both sense and spirit, as if staggering beneath some immense and dark burden, are in such agony that the soul would consider death to be a boon and a relief. "I desire not that he treat me too strongly," says Job, "lest he overwhelm me with the weight of his greatness." Under the stress of this load, feeling alienated and believing that whatever used to uphold her has collapsed along with everything else, the soul is convinced that no one has compassion for her. Job pleaded: "Have pity on me. At least you, my friends, have pity on me, because the hand of the Lord has touched me."

How incredible and sad it is that the soul, in her weakness and impurity, mistakes the soft and gentle hand of God as being heavy and hostile! He does not press down or load up the soul but only touches her and touches her mercifully not to castigate the soul but to grant her favors.

## CHAPTER 6

*Other kinds of pain the soul suffers in this night.*

The joining of two extremes—divine and human—is excruciating. The divine is the purifying contemplation and the human is the soul herself. The divine lays siege upon the soul in order to make her new and to make her divine, stripping her of habitual affections and attachments to the old self to which she had been reconciled. The divine disentangles and dissolves her spiritual substance, absorbing it in deep darkness. In the face of her own misery, the soul feels herself coming undone and melting away in a cruel spiritual death.

It is as if the soul were being swallowed by a beast and disintegrating in the darkness of its belly, like Jonah when he was trapped inside the whale. She must abide in this tomb of dark death until the spiritual resurrection she is hoping for. Although the passion and pain defy description, David offers a glimpse when he says: "The groanings of death encircled me, the pains of hell surrounded me, and in my tribulation I cried out." But what the sorrowing soul feels most acutely is her conviction that God has rejected her and, in abhorrence, tossed her away into the darkness. It is unbearable pain to her to believe that God has forsaken her. "Like the wounded, dead in the sepulchers," says David, "cast away from your hand so that you remember them no more, so I have been placed in the deepest and lowest lake, in the dark shadow of death, and your wrath weighs upon me, and all your waves come crashing in on me."

The soul feels neglected, too, and despised by all creatures, especially by her friends. "You have put far from me my friends and acquaintances; they consider me an abomination," says David. And Jonah says: "You have cast me out into the deep heart of the sea, and the current surrounds me, all its billows and waves pass over me and I say, 'I am cast from the sight of your eyes, yet I shall see again your holy temple' (which he says because this is when God purifies the soul so that she may behold that very thing). The waters engulfed me even unto my soul. The abyss closed in upon me. The open sea covered my head. I went down to the deepest depths of the mountains. The locks of the earth have shut me away forever." These locks stand for the imperfections of the soul, which bar her from enjoying the delicious contemplation.

The majesty of dark contemplation makes the soul feel within herself the other extreme: her own misery. This is one of the sharpest pains she suffers in this purification. The soul feels the utter lack of the three flavors of good which are ordained for the soul's delight: temporal, natural, and spiritual. She finds herself seated in the midst of their opposite evils: the misery of the imperfections, voids in the perceptions of the faculties, and abandonment of the spirit in darkness. As God purifies the sensual and spiritual substance of the soul, in alignment with the exterior and interior faculties, she is thrust into emptiness, abandoned in the dry darkness. The sensory part of the soul is purified in aridity, the faculties in the emptiness of their perceptions, and the spirit in profound obscurity.

In dark contemplation, the soul suffers the suspension of all her natural supports and perceptions, which is terribly painful, like hanging in midair unable to breathe. God is purging the soul, devouring all the imperfect habits and inclinations she has contracted throughout her entire life, as fire consumes the tarnish of metal. Besides this natural and spiritual poverty, she is likely to suffer interior torment from the radical undoing of all the remaining imperfections rooted firmly in the substance of the soul. "I shall gather up the bones and light them on fire. The flesh shall be consumed and the whole composition burned, and the bones shall be destroyed," says Ezechiel. "Place it also empty upon the embers that its metals may heat up and melt, its uncleanness taken away from it, its rust consumed."

Purified in this forge like gold in a crucible, as the Wise Man says, the soul feels as if she herself were coming to an end. David calls out to God: "Save me, Lord, for the waters have come in even unto my soul. I am trapped in the mire of the deep. I have nowhere to stand. I have come unto the depth of the sea and the tempest has overwhelmed me. I have labored in my cry, my throat has become raw and my eyes have failed while I hope in my God."

God greatly humbles the soul now so that he might greatly exalt her later. And he makes it so that when these feelings are quickened in the soul they are soon stilled; otherwise she would die within a few days. The soul is only aware of their vibrancy at intervals. These souls descend into the underworld alive.

———∞∞∞———

# CHAPTER 7

*Considers other burdens and
constraints of the will.*

The soul is startled by sudden realizations of the wickedness in which she has found herself. She is pierced with pain and sees no remedy. Recollecting past prosperity only intensifies the grief. Souls who enter the night of the spirit have already enjoyed many delights in God and have served him with great dedication along the path. Their sorrow is all the greater when they realize how far they are from such goodness, now. They despair of ever being able to enter that realm again.

Job says: "I, who was once wealthy and rich, am suddenly undone and shattered. He has seized my neck and broken me. He has set me up as his target to injure me. He has surrounded me with his spears and wounded all my loins. He has not forgiven me. He has scattered my innards on the earth, breaking me with injury upon injury. He has besieged me like a powerful giant. I have sewn a sack over my skin and covered myself with ashes. My face is swollen with weeping and my eyes are blinded."

And Jeremiah laments: "I am the man who sees my

poverty in the rod of his indignation. He has roused me from slumber and led me into darkness and not into light. He has turned and turned his hand against me all the day. My skin and my flesh he has made old. He has broken my bones. He has built a fence around me and encircled me with bitterness and labor. He has set me in a dark place, as those who are forever dead. He has made a wall around me and against me so that I may not get out; he has made my shackles heavy. And when I would have cried out and pleaded, he shut out my prayers. He has blocked my exits and my ways with square stones. He has thwarted my footsteps. He has become as a lion, hiding in secret places. He has twisted my steps and broken me in pieces. He has made me desolate. He has bent his bow and made of me a mark for his arrow. He has shot into my reins the daughters of his quiver. I have become a source of derision for all the people, of laughter and scorn all the day. He has filled me with bitterness and gotten me drunk on wormwood. One by one he has broken my teeth. He has fed me on ashes. My soul is a stranger to peace. I have forgotten everything that is good. And I said, 'My end, my aim and my hope from the Lord are frustrated and finished. Remember my poverty and excess, the wormwood and bitterness.' I shall be mindful with remembrance and my soul shall languish in pain with me."

Even if it is true that she is very fortunate to have arrived in this place where so many blessings are born, the soul God places in the stormy night of the spirit deserves compassion. Job understands that, "God raises up out of the darkness profound blessings in the soul and turns the shadow of death into light." And David knows that "his light will come to be what his darkness was." Still, the soul suffers terrible pain and is thoroughly dubious about a cure. "She believes," says Jeremiah, "that there is no end to her troubles." And she feels, says David, that "God has hung her in the darkness like the dead of long ago, her spirit in turmoil within her and her heart deeply disturbed."

Added to this pain and suffering is the fact that the soul finds no solace or support in any doctrine or spiritual teacher. This dark night brings solitude and desolation with it. Even though her guides may point out many good reasons for the soul to take comfort in the great blessing signified by her suffering, she cannot believe them. Absorbed and engulfed by awful feelings, clearly discerning her own misery, the soul believes that her teachers say these hopeful things because they do not see and feel what she is seeing and feeling and so cannot possibly understand her. Rather than being consoled by their efforts, her suffering is intensified. She knows there is no hope, no cure, no release from affliction.

And in truth, there is no way out. Until God finishes purifying the soul in the way he desires to do it, no remedy can heal her nor is there relief for her pain. She feels even more helpless when she realizes how little she can do to help herself! She is as powerless as someone imprisoned in a dark dungeon, bound hand and foot, unable to move, who cannot see or feel any favor from above or below. She remains like this until her spirit is humbled, softened, and purified, until she becomes so subtle, so simple, and so refined that she can become one with the spirit of God. In proportion to the degree of union in love that the Beloved, in his mercy, wishes to grant her, the purification is of greater or lesser force and endures for a longer or shorter time.

But if it is authentic it will last for a number of years, however intense it may be. In this process, God grants intervals of relief, in which the dark contemplation ceases to batter the soul (with purgation) and instead shines lovingly upon her (with illumination). This is when the soul becomes like one who has been released from the dungeon and brought up into spaciousness and freedom. She feels the great sweetness of peace and loving friendship with God. She feels the easy flow of abundance in spiritual connection with him.

The soul takes illumination as a sign of the health purgation is bestowing upon her and a foretaste of the plenitude she is hoping for. Sometimes this experience is so profound that the soul thinks all her tribulations must be finished. When the spiritual things that touch the soul are most purely spiritual, they have this extreme quality: when the soul is in trouble, she feels like she will never get out of it and that all her blessings are over; when spiritual blessings come, it seems to the soul that everything difficult is done and that she will never again lack blessings. David reports: "In my abundance I said, 'I shall never be moved.'"

We see that after David's time of prosperity, during which

he declared that he would never be moved, he was indeed moved by many ills and pains. So it is with the soul in the night of spirit. When she finds herself stirred by abundance of spiritual blessings, the root of imperfection and impurity still within her becomes invisible and she may think that her trial has ended. But this thought is rare. Until the spiritual purification is complete, that delicious communion is hardly ever so bountiful that it fully covers up the remaining root. The soul will not cease to feel deep inside herself that something is missing or still needs to be done. This keeps her from relaxing in sweet relief. She feels as if there were an enemy hushed and sleeping within her who might at any moment wake up and wreak havoc.

This is just what happens. When the soul feels most secure and least expects it, purgation drops down upon her all over again and immerses her in yet a deeper degree of darkness, more severe and wrenching than ever before. This one may endure even longer than the last. Once again, the soul believes that all blessings are forever over. Even though the soul basked in bounty after her last trial, convinced she would never suffer again, the experience is not enough to lead her to believe that this second degree of anguish will ever lift or that blessings will ever return. Remember: this powerful conviction arises from the actual perception of the spirit which annihilates within it everything contrary to that belief.

The soul in this purification is so in love with God that she would give a thousand lives for him. Yet this brings her no relief. In fact, it only deepens her pain. Loving God so intensely that nothing else matters, she sees herself as so wretched that God could not possibly love her back. She believes that she neither has nor will ever have within herself anything worthy of his love, seeing cause only to be disdained by God and by all creatures forever. It torments her to survey all the reasons why she deserves to be rejected by him who she so unequivocally loves and longs for.

# CHAPTER 8

*Other pains that afflict the soul in this state.*

Since the dark night is an impediment to the faculties and affections, the soul cannot even lift her thoughts and feelings up to God. She cannot pray. It seems to the soul, as it did to Jeremiah, that God has placed "a cloud in front of me through which prayer may not pass." Remember when Jeremiah says: "He has blocked my exits and my ways with square stones." If the soul does try to pray, she prays with so little energy and juice that she doubts God can even hear her or is paying any attention to her. "When I cry out and invoke him," says Jeremiah, "he excludes my prayer."

The truth is, this is no time to talk to God. Instead, the soul should, as Jeremiah recommends, "put her mouth in the dust, that there may come to her some actual hope." She must suffer her purification patiently. It is God who is now working in the soul, passively. She herself can do nothing. She cannot pray or attend to any spiritual things. She is even less successful in dealing with worldly business. She sometimes slips into such altered states and such profound forgetfulness that long periods can pass during which the soul has no idea what she is thinking or doing. Nor does she know what she is going to do next. No matter how much she may want to, she cannot focus on the task at hand.

Not only is the mind purged of its light and the will of its attachments, but the memory is stripped of cognitive content. David says: "I was annihilated and I knew not." The "unknowing" refers to these confusions and lapses of memory. The distraction and absentmindedness is caused by the interior recollection in which contemplation is absorbing the soul. The duration of withdrawal from creature-perceptions and spirit-attachments corresponds to the intensity of the contemplation. The more simply and purely the divine light strikes the soul, the more radically it eradicates her particular attachments to and perceptions of things of above and things of below. The less purely this light shines, the less it darkens and deprives the soul.

Doesn't it seem incredible that the brighter and purer the divine and supernatural light, the darker it is to the soul? Isn't it amazing that the less bright and pure it is, the less dark it is to the soul? This paradox makes sense if we consider the teachings of the Philosopher, who proved that the clearer and more manifest are supernatural things in themselves, the darker they are to our minds.

Consider common, natural light: a sunbeam shines through a window. The freer the air is from little specks of dust, the less clearly we see the ray of light. The more motes that are floating in the air, the more clearly the sunbeam appears to our eye. This is because light itself is invisible. Light is the means by which the things it strikes are perceived. It is seen only by its reflection in them. If the light did not shine upon these things, it would not be seen and neither would they. In a way, there is more darkness where a ray of light is present because it absorbs and obscures any other light.

This is just what the divine ray of contemplation does to the soul. Smiting her with divine light, contemplation transcends the soul's very nature. It darkens and deprives her of all the natural perceptions and affections she used to experience with her own natural light. Darkened and emptied, the soul is purified and illumined by divine light. Like the ray of light that remains invisible even in the middle of a room as long as it has nothing to bump up against, so this divine light is invisible to the purified soul and she thinks she is in darkness. Yet when this spiritual light strikes the soul and finds something to reflect, the soul sees and understands herself much more clearly than she did before she entered these dark places. It does not matter if her spiritual insight is tiny or vast, if it is about perfection or imperfection, if it is a judgment of truth or illusion. Easily recognizing her own limitations, the soul can now clearly perceive spiritual light.

This light is so simple, so pure, so sweeping! No particular thing in the intellect, either natural or divine, affects it or restricts it. The faculties of the soul have been emptied and annihilated of all such apprehensions. Now, with great ease and plenitude, the soul perceives and penetrates anything that is offered to her from above or below. The Apostle says that "the spiritual person sees into all things, unto the deepest things of God." What simple general wisdom! "It touches everywhere because of its purity," says the Wise Man. The divine spirit cannot be particularized by any desire or object in the mind.

# CHAPTER 9

*Although this night darkens the spirit,*
*it illumines and fills her with light.*

Even though this holy night darkens the spirit, it does so only to light up everything. Even though it humbles her and makes her miserable, it is only to raise her up and exalt her. Even though it impoverishes her, emptying her of natural inclinations, it is only so that she will reach out for the divine and freely enjoy the fruits of all things, of above and of below.

For elements to blend into compounds and natural entities, they have to be devoid of any particular color, fragrance, or flavor. Only then can they commingle with all flavors, fragrances, and colors. The spirit, too, must be simple, pure, and naked of all attachments. Only then can she freely partake—with fullness of spirit—of the divine wisdom. Through her purity, she tastes the eminent sweetness of all things. Without this purification, she would be unable to feel or taste the delectability of these abundant spiritual delights. Bound by even one remaining attachment to any particular object and she will be incapable of feeling or tasting the subtle and intimate sweetness of the spirit of love, which holds within itself all sweetnesses.

The Children of Israel could not taste the delicate bread of the angels in the desert, which was the manna the scriptures say contained all flavors and became the favorite taste each one most desired. This is because they still held onto the memory of the meats they loved in Egypt. In the same way, the spirit that is still affected by desire or by some particular concept or by any other perception is unable to taste the delights of spiritual freedom. The desires, feelings, and perceptions of the perfected spirit are entirely different from the natural ones. They are exalted. They are divine. For the spirit to be able to hold them means that all natural inclinations have to be eradicated, because two opposites cannot coexist in a single subject.

And so, if the soul is going to pass into this greatness, the dark night of contemplation has to annihilate her, first. Her inferior tendencies must come undone. The night sets her down in darkness and aridity, in emptiness and strife. The light she will ultimately be given is the highest degree of divine light. It utterly transcends the soul's natural light. It has no home in the intellect. For the mind to reach the divine light and meld with it and, in a state of perfection, to become divine, the dark contemplation must first obliterate its natural light. The mind has to be plunged into darkness. This darkness will last as long as it needs to pull the mind up out of those old ruts it has been stuck in for so long. Then the illumination of divine light can take over. Since the old ways of understanding were natural to the mind, the darkness the soul endures here will be especially profound and painful. It seems impenetrable. The soul feels this darkness in the deepest substance of her spirit.

The love that the divine union will pour upon the soul is divine love. It is very subtle, delicate, and spiritual. It is interior. It surpasses every feeling and inclination of the will and overrides every desire. And so the will, too, must first be purged of all feelings and preferences before it can taste the divine sweetness and exalted delight of the union of love, which does not belong to the will. The soul is thoroughly tempered by the fire of this dark contemplation, cleansed of every kind of demon, like the heart of the fish Tobias set on the coals. Her disposition is purified and simplified. Her palate is purged and healed so that it can taste the sublime and wondrous textures of divine love. All obstacles are driven out. The soul is transformed.

Connection with God fills the soul with a certain splendor and glory. She overflows with blessings springing from delights that far surpass any she could attain naturally. This is the stuff of union. This is where the dark night is leading the soul. This is what it is getting her ready for. The natural being is not pure enough or strong enough to receive these delights. Isaiah says: "Eye has not seen nor has ear heard nor has it entered into the heart of humanity that which God has prepared."

And so the soul is brought first into emptiness and poverty of spirit. She is purged of every natural support, consolation, and perception, from above or from below. Only then, radically empty, stripped naked of the old self, is she truly poor of spirit. Only then can she live that new and blessed life. This is the dark night. This is what yields union with God.

A delicious feeling will wash over the soul, accompanied by a generous knowing of all things, human and divine. These things do not fall into the old realm of common sense or ordinary knowledge. The soul looks upon these things with eyes as different from the eyes of the past as spirit is from sense and the divine from the human. When it comes to regular natural experiences, the soul is cropped and weatherbeaten. This purifying contemplation brings the soul great anguish. Her memory is deprived of everything pleasant and peaceful. The soul is overcome by this inner sense of exile. Everything feels strange and different from what it used to be.

This night draws the spirit away from her customary feeling for things. It brings her a sense of the divine. This is alien to human ways. Her suffering seems to transport her beyond herself. Sometimes the soul even wonders if she might be under a spell, captivated. She wanders around amazed by the things she sees and hears. Everything seems so peculiar, even though nothing has really changed. This is because the soul is becoming a stranger to herself. She does not have access to common sense or ordinary knowledge anymore. Thus annihilated, she can be informed by the divine. This is a thing belonging more to the next life than to this one.

The soul suffers the pain of spiritual purification so that

she can be quickened by the divine inflow and regenerated in the life of the spirit. As Isaiah says: "By your presence, Lord, we have conceived, and we have been as in the pains of labor, and we have brought forth the spirit of salvation."

The soul needs to give up on the peace of her past. The night of contemplation is preparing her for inner tranquility so exquisite that, as the scriptures say, "it surpasses all understanding." That other peace was really no peace at all, because it was shrouded in imperfections. It only seemed that way to a soul following her own inclinations. She felt like she had, in fact, attained a double peace: peace of sense and peace of spirit. She saw herself filled with holy abundance. But this sensual and spiritual peace is still imperfect and needs to be purified. It must be shattered and swept away. This is Jeremiah's lament expressing the misery of that heavy night: "My soul is withdrawn and removed from peace."

It is a painful upheaval, stirring up a myriad of fears and delusions that battle inside the soul. Her perception of the misery in which she finds herself leads the soul to suspect that she is hopelessly lost and that all blessings, too, are lost forever. The sorrowing and sighing of her spirit are so profound that they turn into a mighty roaring and bellowing. She is so powerfully wracked by pain that sometimes she cries out and dissolves in tears (if she even still has the strength needed for weeping). This kind of relief, however, is a rare thing.

In a Psalm, David says: "I was unbearably afflicted and humbled. I roared with the groaning of my heart." This roaring gives voice to unspeakable suffering. Sometimes the soul is pierced by a sudden awareness of the wretchedness she finds herself immersed in. Pain rises up to engulf her. I know of no other words to describe this trial than those of the saintly Job: "Even as the overflowing of the waters, so is my roaring." Just as sometimes the waters rise, filling up and inundating an entire landscape, so this feeling and its accompanying roaring grow so vast that they overwhelm and penetrate everything, invading all the soul's deepest inclinations and energies with a spiritual agony beyond measure.

Such is the work this night does inside the soul. It covers up all hope for the light of day. The Prophet Job says: "In the night my mouth is pierced by grief, and they that feed upon me do not sleep." The mouth represents the will that is punctured by a suffering that never rests, that does not let up, that tears the soul to shreds. The doubts and fears that stab her are never-ending. Job says that the soul is withering within herself, now, her innermost parts boiling away. The battle within her is deep, just as the peace she is waiting for will be deep; her pain private and delicate, because the love she will have is just as intimate and refined. The more masterful a work of art, the more careful must be the labor. The energy committed to construction is reflected in the solidity of a building.

In her journey through this purifying night, the soul will eventually come to enjoy a state of perfection overflowing with countless gifts and virtues. But first she is required to suffer the general withdrawal and deprivation of these wonders. This makes her feel empty and impoverished. It is absolutely necessary for the soul to see herself as so far removed from these wonderful things that she cannot possibly persuade herself they will ever come back to her. All she can believe, like Jeremiah, is that everything excellent is over: "I have forgotten good things."

But why is it that the light of contemplation assaults the soul so violently, creating such negative effects? Isn't the light of contemplation so gentle and kind that there is nothing more the soul could possibly desire? Isn't this the same light of contemplation that will unify the soul and in which she will discover all the blessings of the perfect state she yearns for?

Remember: there is nothing about contemplation or the inflow of the divine that is in itself painful; rather, these conditions bring sweetness and delight. It is that the soul at this stage of her purifying journey still suffers from a little bit of weakness and imperfection. She still has certain inclinations that keep her from being receptive to these blessings. When the divine light strikes her, she suffers. She is not quite ready.

# CHAPTER 10

*Using a comparison to fully explain this purification.*

Let's look at this loving knowledge and divine light like fire. Fire transforms wood into fire. When fire touches wood, the first thing it does is that it begins to dry the wood out. It drives away moisture, causing the wood to shed the tears it has held inside itself. Then the wood blackens, turning dark and ugly; it may even give off a bad odor. Little by little, the fire desiccates the wood, bringing out and driving away all those dark and unsavory accidents that are contrary to the nature of fire. Finally, heating up and enkindling the wood from the outside, the fire transforms the wood into itself, rendering the wood as beautiful as the fire is.

The wood is left without any interests or activities of its own. What it has is its weight, which is heavier, and its quantity, which is denser than the fire. Now the wood has inside itself the properties of fire and it performs the work of fire. It is dry and it dries. It is hot and it heats. It is bright and it illumines. It is much lighter than before. Fire creates all these properties and yields all these effects.

This is how it is with the divine flame of contemplative love. Before it transforms and unites the soul within itself, it purifies her of all contrary qualities. It darkens her, blackens her. It dries up her impurities. She feels worse than ever—uglier, more loathsome. This divine cleansing stirs up all the negativities and nasty inclinations which the soul did not even notice before because they were so deeply rooted and grounded within her.

As foul humors are expelled and annihilated, they are brought to the light, clearly illumined by the dark light of divine illumination. Actually, the soul is no worse than she was before—either within herself or in her connection with God. It's just that she sees in herself what she never saw before, and it makes her feel terrible. She is convinced that not only does she deserve God's contempt but that he does, in fact, despise her.

The very light and loving wisdom that transforms and unites the soul with itself in the end is what purifies and prepares the soul in the beginning. Fire transforms wood by incorporating it into itself only by first preparing it for this transformation.

The soul feels her pain to be coming from her own weakness and not from divine wisdom. As the Wise Man says: "All good things come to the soul together with her." Without this purification, the soul cannot receive the divine light, sweetness, and delight, in the same way that the wood cannot be transformed by the fire that acts upon it until the fire itself prepares it. And so the soul suffers deeply. Ecclesiastes describes what he had to endure to be able to unite with wisdom and revel in it: "My soul has wrestled in her and my insides were thrown into confusion acquiring her; therefore I shall possess a good possession."

Impure souls suffer. If they had no imperfections, the spiritual fire would be powerless over them. Imperfections are the fuel it ignites. Once they are consumed, there is nothing left to burn. When the imperfections are gone, the soul's suffering is over and what remains is joy.

As the soul is purged and purified in this fire of love, she becomes more and more deeply enkindled in love, just as the wood burns hotter as the fire prepares it more completely. The soul, however, does not always feel the enkindling of love. Sometimes this contemplative light shines more intensely upon the soul, giving her the chance to notice and even appreciate the good work happening inside her. Like a blacksmith who pauses in his labor to withdraw the iron from the forge and examine the craftsmanship, the soul is able to see the good that was not apparent to her in the middle of the work itself. It is only when the flame stops wounding the wood that the wood discovers how thoroughly it has been ignited.

And then, after having been been relieved of her pain, the soul suffers all over again, more deeply and intensely than before. External imperfections are purified at first; then the fire of love sweeps over the soul again to purify the internal fuel still left to be consumed. The suffering of the soul grows more intimate, subtle, and spiritual, reflecting the deep-rooted intimacy, subtlety, and spirituality of the imperfections burning deep inside her. This is the way fire treats wood. The more profoundly the flame penetrates the log, the more powerfully it behaves, getting the wood ready to be possessed at its very core.

Why does it seem to the soul that all blessings have fallen away and that she is filled with badness? Why is she is aware of nothing but her own bitterness? When wood burns, nothing else can touch it but that all-consuming fire. But when relief comes, the soul will rejoice deep inside herself, because it is deep inside her that the purification has happened.

Even though the soul's joy during these intervals is ample—so ample that she cannot imagine ever suffering again—she also has this feeling that some deep root remains, and she cannot help but conclude that her trials will resume. This foreboding prevents the soul from fully appreciating her reprieve. As soon as the soul begins to wonder about the threat of another wave of purification, she is besieged all over again. That innermost part of the soul still to be purged and enlightened cannot hide behind the already-purified part.

In wood, too, there is a clear difference between the innermost portion still to be enkindled and the portion that has already burned. When purification descends upon the soul in her deepest recesses, it is no wonder that she starts thinking again that all good is gone and the blessings will never come back. Engulfed by these internal passions, she is blind to any external benevolence.

It would be good to leave these sad things now and go on to explore the fruit of the soul's tears and the joyous properties of the dark night. This is what the soul begins to sing about in the second line:

*"Inflamed by love-longing . . ."*

# CHAPTER 11

*Begins to explain the second line of the first song
and tells how the soul, harvesting the
fruit of these rigorous challenges,
finds herself madly in love with the divine.*

The soul is singing about the fire of love. In this night of painful contemplation, the soul is ignited. Although the burning in some ways resembles what unfolded in the sensory part of the soul, in other ways it is as different as the soul is from the body. This is a love that blazes in the spirit. In the middle of her dark predicament, the soul feels herself vividly wounded by the flaming blade of divine love. And she is stirred by an inkling of God's presence, even though her mind sits in darkness and she does not understand anything.

This spiritual conflagration arouses love's passion, and the spirit finds herself madly in love with God. This is an infused love. It is an action of God, working on the soul passively. It enters and takes hold of her, although the soul gives this love her consent. It is the love of God, drawing the soul toward union with him. It kindles the heated mood of love, which the soul calls fire.

All the soul's old desires have been incapacitated and shut down. She is incapable of being satisfied by anything of heaven or of earth. When this love shows up in the soul, it finds her ready to be wounded and united with love itself. In this dark purification, God weans the soul from all other cravings by withdrawing them and gathering them all inside himself. In this way, he strengthens the soul so that she is better equipped to receive the powerful union of divine love.

Through burning purification, God is beginning to give this love to the soul. And the soul is beginning to love him in return, with tremendous force, engaging her purest sensual and spiritual desires. Such love is only possible when the appetites are no longer scattered by their inclination toward any other thing. David said to God: "I will keep my strength for you." That is, I will reserve all the capacity and all the desire and all the energy of my faculties for God. There is no other object of pleasure than him.

Consider how vast and mighty this fire of love is that burns in the spirit. God collects all the functions of the soul—sensual and spiritual—and commits the power and virtue of this harmonious whole to the flames of love. And so the soul, not excluding for a minute anything human from this love, truly fulfills the first commandment: "You shall love your God with all your soul and all your heart and all your mind and all your strength." Once the soul has been struck and wounded by this burning love, all her energies and desires are driven into this single passion. How can we fathom the stirrings and impulses of all these energies and desires? The soul can tell that she is seriously wounded and lit on fire by this powerful love, but she still cannot grasp it or get any satisfaction from it. She remains in darkness and doubt. As David says, the soul is like a starving dog wandering around the city, howling and moaning, yearning to be filled with love.

The touch of this divine love dries up the spirit and enkindles the soul. The urge to satisfy her thirst for God is so strong that she turns a thousand circles inside herself and yearns for him in a thousand ways. "My soul thirsts for you; in how many ways does my soul long for you!" says David in a Psalm. Another version goes like this: "My soul thirsts for you. My soul loses itself and dies for you."

And so the soul says in this line that she is "inflamed by the longings of love." In everything she does, in all the thoughts revolving inside her, in all her activities and in every event that arises, in her desire and in the suffering that comes from desire, the soul is loving God all the time, everywhere. She does not find peace anywhere. She feels this longing like an inflamed wound. Job says: "As the deer desires shade and the laborer desires the end of his labor, so have I had empty months and numbered to myself long and wearisome nights. If I lie down to sleep I say, 'When will I get up?' Then I wait till evening and I am filled with sorrows until the dark of night."

Everything cramps the soul. She does not fit inside herself. She does not fit in heaven or on earth. She is lost in sorrow until the spiritual darkness falls, which is what Job is talking about. The agony is not mollified by one shred of hope for any spiritual light or for anything good whatsoever.

This burning love compounds the soul's suffering by engulfing her in spiritual darkness and plaguing her with doubts and fears, by inflaming, stimulating, and stirring her with a wondrous wound of love. Isaiah says: "My soul desired you in the night," that is, in misery, "yet within my spirit," he goes onto say, "at my deepest core, until the morning I will wait for you," which expresses the anxiety of love-longing.

Still, in the middle of dark grief, the soul senses a certain companion deep inside herself. This presence keeps the soul company and fortifies her. In fact, if her burden of painful darkness was removed, the soul would feel alone—empty and weak. The power and value of the soul came to her when she was besieged by the dark fire of love. When the siege lifts, the darkness, potency, and heat of love fall away and the soul feels like she is left with nothing, bereft.

# CHAPTER 12

*How this awesome night of divine wisdom*
*purifies and illumines human souls with the*
*same light that purifies and illumines the angels.*

As the night of loving fire purifies the soul in darkness, in darkness it enkindles her. The pure of heart are called blessed in the Gospel. He could just as well say that the pure of heart are in love, because blessedness comes only from love. Purity of heart is nothing other than the loving grace of God.

It is love that infuses mystical wisdom; God never bestows wisdom without love. "He sent fire into my bones and he taught me," says Jeremiah. And David says: "God's wisdom is silver smelted in the fire," that is, in the purifying fire of love. Contemplation infuses the soul with both love and wisdom in proportion to her capacity and her need. It illumines the soul and purges her of ignorance, which is what the Wise Man says it did to him too.

The very same divine wisdom that purifies and illumines these souls cleanses the angels of ignorance and gives them understanding. This wisdom flows from God from the first levels to the last and on into the human realm. As it explains in the scriptures, all the work of the angels and all their inspirations originate in God. The angels pass these inspirations and accomplishments swiftly from one to another. This transmission acts like a sunbeam passing through a series of windows all lined up in a row. Even though the ray of light shines through them all, each window communicates the light to the next in a modified form, based on the nature of the glass. The intensity of the transmission is a measure of how far away or near the window is from the sun.

And so the nearer the higher spirits are to God, the more thoroughly are they purged and clarified by sweeping purification. The lowest of these spirits receive the faintest, most remote concentration of illumination. The human being, which is the last in line to receive the transmission of God's loving contemplation, experiences it according to his own nature: limited and painful.

Angels are pure spirits. They are ready for the inflow of love. Divine light illumines the angels by clarifying and softening them; it illumines the human soul by plunging her into darkness. It is the soul's own weakness and impurity that torments her, like when the sun blazes on a diseased eye. The fire of love fills the soul with passion and pain. It refines and spiritualizes her. Eventually, she will be ready to receive the loving inflow gently, like the angels do. Until then, as the soul takes in the contemplation and loving knowledge, it upsets her. The love stirs her longing for love.

The soul does not always feel the fire of urgent yearning. When spiritual purification first starts, all the energy of divine fire is directed toward drying out and preparing the wood (the soul) rather than toward generating heat. But as time passes, the fire begins to radiate warmth and the soul starts to feel the burning of love.

As the darkness purges the mind, it also delicately and delightfully wounds it with the light of sacred knowledge. This "loving mystical theology" ignites the will with a wondrous fever. Divine fire burns inside the passive will like a vital flame. Because this knowledge is a living knowledge, the fire feels like a living fire. David says in a Psalm: "My heart grew hot within me and my knowing enkindled a certain fire." The fire of love which unites the mind with the will brings the soul richness and delight. It carries a taste of the divine, a hint of the perfect union of love the soul has longed for. No one receives such a sublime touch of God's love without having suffered many trials and extensive purification. Lighter touches are more common and they do not require such suffering.

When God infuses the soul with these blessings, it is possible for the will to love without the mind understanding, or for the mind to understand without the will loving. The dark night of infused contemplation is made up of divine light and love, just as fire radiates both light and heat. Sometimes this loving light strikes the will and ignites it with love, leaving the mind in darkness, while at other times it illumines the mind with understanding and abandons the will in aridity. It is like feeling the warmth of the fire without seeing its light or seeing its light but not feeling the heat. It is up to God how he will infuse the soul.

# CHAPTER 13

*Other delightful effects of the dark night
of contemplation on the soul.*

Sometimes the contemplative night pierces the darkness and illumines the soul. It quietly conveys mystical knowledge to the mind and leaves the will dry, uninvolved in the union. The simple serenity that comes of this transmission is ineffable: now the experience of God feels like this; now it feels like that.

Sometimes this dark night of contemplation strikes the mind and the will simultaneously, enkindling a sublime and powerful love. Remember: once the mind has been purified, it is more likely to come into harmony with the will. To the extent that both are purified, the union is that much deeper. But before the soul attains to such a place of purification, it is more common for her to experience the touch of fire in the will than the touch of understanding in the mind.

Here is a question: If the faculties of mind and will are being purified together, why does the purifying contemplation make itself felt more commonly as an igniting of love in the will than as any kind of intellectual understanding?

Here is an answer: the will is free. This is a passive love, more of a burning passion than an act of free will. The warmth of love hits the substance of the soul, and the affections are moved in spite of themselves. An act of will is really only an act of will if it is free. This passion of love subdues the will and instills it with that passion. It steals away the freedom of the will and holds it captive. The impetus of love is that powerful. So we call this an enkindling of love in the will because the passionate love arouses desire, which takes up the work of the free will. The receptive capacity of the mind can only receive the naked, passive knowledge of the divine when it is purified. Until that purification is complete, the soul experiences the touch of understanding more rarely than she feels the passion of love. On the other hand, it is not necessary for the will to be fully purged of its own passions in order to feel the love. In fact, its own passion even helps it to feel impassioned divine love.

This burning thirst of love belongs to the spirit. It is very different from the love that inflamed the senses, before. The senses participate in this love, because they share all the work of the spirit, but the source of the intensity of thirst resides in the higher part of the soul. The spirit feels the lack of what it longs for in an acutely spiritual way. The suffering that the senses experience here, though incomparably greater than it was during the night of sense, does not even come close to approaching the agony in the spirit when the soul becomes aware deep inside herself that she is missing that immeasurable good.

Remember: it takes a while for the fire of love to catch. The soul might not feel it when the spiritual night first falls. But from the very outset of this night, the soul is touched by love-longings. Sometimes this is felt as deep regard; at other times it is a burning passion. From the beginning, God awakens in the soul, at the very least, a singular esteem for him. This reverence can be so intense that the most severe trials and tribulations of the night arise from the soul's anguish in thinking that she has lost God and that he has abandoned her. It seems that the greatest suffering the soul undergoes here is this very fear. If only the soul could be sure that all is not lost, that her suffering is for the best, and that God is not mad at her, then all this pain would not even bother her! Instead, the soul would rejoice in the knowledge that God is making good use of her. Her loving esteem for God is so great that the soul would actually be happy to suffer all these things—in fact to die over and over again—just to please him.

When the fire of love joins with the esteem the soul already feels for God, the warmth of love strengthens her and makes her brave. It intensifies her longing for him. She would do whatever it took—no matter how crazy—to encounter the one she loves. The power of love and desire intoxicates her and makes her bold; the soul would do anything for God, oblivious to any potential consequences.

Mary Magdalene, in spite of her past, paid no attention to the men at the banquet. It made no difference to her if they were prominent or common. She did not consider whether it was proper to go sobbing and shedding tears among the guests. Her only concern was to reach the one who had wounded her soul and set it on fire. No, she could not wait for a more appropriate time! The intoxication of love gives the soul crazy courage. Knowing that her Beloved was sealed in a tomb by an enormous rock, surrounded by guards posted just in case the disciples would try to steal his body, Mary did not let anything stand in the way of her going out before daybreak to anoint him with ointments. Finally, the inebriating power of her love-longing compelled Mary to ask a man she thought was a gardener if he had stolen him and, if he had, where he had put him so that she could take him back. She did not pause to consider that, by the light of sound judgment, her question sounded ridiculous. Obviously, if the man had stolen him, he would not have confessed this, and he certainly would not have led her to him.

The power and intensity of love have this quality. Love makes everything seem possible. Love believes everyone must feel this same passion. Love cannot understand how anyone could waste their time doing anything other than seeking the Beloved. When the bride went out in search of her Beloved through the streets and plazas, assuming everybody else must be up to the same thing, she told them all that if they found him they should please inform him that she was suffering with love for him. Mary's love was so fervent that she thought if only the gardener would tell her where her Beloved was hidden she would go and get him, no matter how difficult the challenge.

This is the power of love-longing, once the soul has advanced in spiritual purification. In the darkness of night, the wounded soul rises up in response to the affections of the will. Like a lioness or a she-bear that goes looking for her lost cubs, the wounded soul goes anxiously forth in search of her God. In darkness, she feels only his absence. She feels like she is dying with love for him. In fact, such is the nature of this impatient love that she cannot endure one more minute without either gaining the object of her desire or dying. This is the yearning Rachel had for children when she said to Jacob: "Give me children; otherwise I will die."

Even though in the midst of this purifying darkness the soul considers herself to be wretched and unworthy, she still has the energy and daring to go out and find union with God! Love gives the soul strength to love truly. And it is love's nature to seek to be connected to, made equal with, and assimilated into the object of love and to be perfected in love's goodness. The soul that has not yet achieved perfection in the union of love hungers and thirsts for what she still lacks. The power of love impassions the will and makes it bolder. But the mind is not yet illumined and remains in darkness. The soul still feels miserable.

Why doesn't this divine light, which is always radiance to the soul, illumine the soul the instant it strikes her but instead causes darkness and difficulty? Remember: the darkness and wickedness the soul experiences when the light strikes her are not caused by the light; they belong to the soul herself. What the light is doing is illumining her so she can see her imperfections. And this light illumines her from the very beginning. At first, however, she can only see what is nearest to her, in fact what is inside of her, which is the shadow of her own misery. It is by the grace of God that she gets to perceive this, now. She did not see these things before because the supernatural light had not yet shone on her like this. It is only early on that the soul feels this darkness and insignificance. After being purified by the realization of these things, the soul will have eyes to see the great blessings of the divine light. Once all the soul's shadows and impurities are driven out, the tremendous benefits she is gaining through this sweet night of contemplation become clearer.

God grants the soul in this state the favor of cleansing and healing her. He washes clean both sense and spirit with the bitter solvent of purification. By darkening the interior faculties and emptying them of all objects, God frees the soul from her imperfect inclinations toward sensory and spiritual things. He restrains the natural forces of the soul so that they weaken and dry up; he refines them. No soul can accomplish this work by herself.

In this way, God makes the soul die to all that is not inherently of God. When the soul is stripped bare of her old skin, God clothes her afresh. Her youth is revitalized like the eagle's. She is clothed in newness of being. She is created, as the Apostle says, according to God. It is nothing less than illumination of the natural mind by supernatural light so that, through union with what is divine, the mind, too, becomes divine. It is nothing less than an infusing of the will with the love of God so that it is no longer other than divine itself and, made one with the divine will and love, loves divinely. It is nothing less than a divine conversion and alteration of the memory, the inclinations, and the desires so that they conform to God's.

And so this soul will be a soul of heaven. Heavenly. More divine than human.

God does all this good work in the soul by enkindling her love-longing for God alone. This is why the soul adds this third line to her song:

*"O exquisite risk!—*
*Undetected I slipped away."*

# CHAPTER 14

*An explanation of the last few lines
of the first song of the soul.*

The exquisite risk the soul has taken now inspires her to sing:

*Undetected I slipped away.
My house, at last, grown still.*

This metaphor describes a lover who sneaks out of the house under the cloak of darkness when everybody is asleep so that no one can thwart her plan. The soul has to leave home to accomplish the rare and heroic deed of becoming one with her divine Beloved, who is only found in solitude. The bride cries: "Who will give you to me, my brother, that I might find you alone outside and communicate my love to you?"

To reach her desired goal, the soul in love needs to go out at night when all her household members are sleeping. These are all the soul's lower functions and appetites, which are quelled by the night. They are not in favor of the soul's freedom. When they are awake, they invariably try to stand in the way of the soul taking off in search of the one she longs for. It says in the Gospel that the most dangerous people are the ones who live in our own home. The natural functions and activities have to be put to sleep in this night so that they cannot interfere and the soul is free to receive the blessing of union in love with God. The soul's natural faculties hinder rather than assist her in reaping the harvest that is the union of love. There is not a single natural ability capable of producing the supernatural blessings with which God passively infuses the soul, secretly, and in silence. All the faculties receive this infusion. But to receive it, they have to be passive. They cannot get in the way with their awkward functions and banal inclinations.

The exquisite risk begins once the soul finds all the members of her household asleep. It is God who has put all the passions and appetites—both sensual and spiritual—to bed. This is how the soul is able to escape "unnoticed." Once these elements are stilled, the soul can go out into the darkness of night toward the spiritual union of God's perfect love. Lost in their lowly, natural unconsciousness, these elements will not see a thing. Unimpeded, the soul can go out from herself.

Oh, what an exquisite risk it is for the soul to be freed from the house of the senses! I doubt anyone other than the soul who experiences it can know how happy it makes her. This is when the soul begins to realize the wretched servitude and all the misery she suffered when she was at the mercy of her faculties and desires. Now she sees how it is the life of the spirit that embodies true freedom and boundless richness.

# CHAPTER 15

*An explanation of the second verse.*

Just because I have endured the storms of anguish, doubt, and fear, the soul sings, do not think that I have for a minute run the risk of being lost. Quite the opposite; in the darkness of this night I have found myself.

In the night, I sneak away from my enemies, who are perpetually impeding my progress. In the darkness, I change my clothes and disguise myself with garments of three different colors. I leave by a very secret passageway that no one in the house knows about, concealing myself so that I can accomplish my goal.

I am especially secure in this night of purification because my appetites, inclinations, and passions have been put to sleep, humbled, and stilled. Awake and vitalized, they would never consent to this journey!

I am

*"Secure in the darkness . . ."*

CHAPTER 16

An explanation of how the soul walks
securely in the darkness.

What is happening to the soul at this point? The light of the contemplative night purifies her sensual and spiritual functions and desires. By darkening their natural light, it illumines them supernaturally. The night lulls her senses and her intellect to sleep. It deprives them of the ability to find gratification in anything. It ties up the imagination so that it cannot formulate a complete thought.

Once the discursive mind shuts down in the darkness, the will follows; it dries up and quits. All the faculties become empty and useless. A dense and heavy cloud hangs over the soul. She feels miserable in her separation from God. And yet, it is in this very "darkness" that the soul is able to travel "securely" to him.

The only things that usually motivate a soul to move or change are her natural impulses. She either wants something too much or she does not understand something enough. These excesses and absences compel the soul to do things that are not good for her. Once the faculties are confounded, the soul can no longer be impeded by them. That is when she is liberated from herself and from her other adversaries: the world and the Spirit of Evil. When the natural functions and inclinations of the soul are quelled, her foes have no way to wage war on her.

And so, through emptiness and darkness, the soul walks surefooted. As the Prophet says, the soul's ruination comes only from herself (from her sensual and spiritual attachments) while her goodness, says God, comes from me alone [Hos. 13:9]. Once the soul is obstructed from following the paths that lead to trouble, her faculties and desires will deliver her to union with God, where they are themselves transfigured and made divine.

Look closely inside the darkness. See how undistracted the soul is by irrelevant or harmful things, now. See how secure she is, safe from pride and presumption. See how she is unmoved by false joy. By walking in darkness, the soul not only avoids getting lost, but she makes excellent progress because she is evolving in virtue.

Here is a question: If the things of God are inherently good, why does God darken the faculties and inclinations so that the soul can find even less satisfaction in holy things than she finds in those other distractions?

The answer: the soul's natural functions and inclinations are still impure. If God were to give the soul a taste of supernatural delight, she would only be able to experience it in an impure way. As the Philosopher says, whatever is received comes in according to the nature of the receiver. The natural faculties have to be darkened to receive the divine. They need to be weaned from attachment, purged of impurity, annihilated. Only when the old self dies is the soul, strengthened and tempered, ready to experience and savor the sacred.

Unless the Master of Lights is communicating directly to the human desire and free will, the soul will not taste him spiritually. It does not matter how committed her natural faculties are to experiencing God or how much pleasure she derives from her intentions. Spiritual blessings do not go out from human to divine; they come from the divine to the human.

How many people have an inclination toward God, a taste for spiritual things, and a dedication to apply all their energies to connecting with him and even find satisfaction in these practices and yet do all this in a thoroughly human way? These people have the natural ability to direct their faculties and inclinations toward anything at all. Their emphasis on spiritual things is no different than their attachment to things of the world. Sometimes the way the soul moves in response to communication from God is natural and human; other times it is purely spiritual. Sometimes it's both. But if the soul is going to be moved by God directly, her natural operations first have to be pacified, weakened, and put to rest.

Oh, spiritual soul! When you see that your desires are darkened, your inclinations dried up, and your faculties incapacitated, do not be disturbed. Consider it grace. God is freeing you from yourself. He is taking the matter from your hands. No matter how well these hands may have served you, they are still clumsy and unclean. Never before could you labor as effectively as you can now when you put down your burden and let God take your hand and guide you through the darkness as though you were blind, leading you to a place you do not know. Who cares how good your hands and feet may be?

The soul has no clue that she is advancing on her path. When new gifts come to her, they come in a way that she cannot understand. Since she has never before had this experience which drives her out of herself, dazzles her, and takes her on a wild detour off her normal path, she thinks she is getting lost and losing ground. And it's true. She is losing herself to all that she has ever known or tasted. She is walking a road of entirely new flavors and new knowledge.

To get to an unknown land by unknown roads, a traveler cannot allow himself to be guided by his old experience. He has to doubt himself and seek the guidance of others. There is no way he can reach new territory and know it truly unless he abandons familiar trails. When an apprentice is learning new details about his trade, he works in darkness. What he already knows is of no use to him. If he were to cling to the old methods, he would not make any progress.

The soul is making the most progress when she is traveling through the deepest darkness, knowing nothing. Since it is God that is the master and guide of the blind soul, she can rejoice. Once she understands this, she can consider herself to be "secure in the darkness."

This is a soul that has been suffering. Suffering is more fruitful than pleasure. It is in suffering and in stillness that God strengthens the soul. When she is active and satisfied, she practices nothing more than her own inclinations and weaknesses. In suffering, the soul evolves in virtue and purity. She wakes up and grows wiser.

The dark night of contemplation envelops the soul in itself and draws her near to God. The dark light of wisdom frees the soul and protects her from all that does not evoke remembrance of God. The soul is taking a remedy to restore her health and the cure is God. And so God-the-healer restricts her diet to abstinence from all things; he makes her lose her appetite for them all. God treats the soul the way a loving family tends an adored member who is sick. They keep him inside to protect him from the harsh weather. They try not to disturb him with the sound of their footsteps or their whispering. They feed him moderate and wholesome food, even if it is not very tasty.

The closer the soul comes to God, the more profound the darkness she feels. It is like someone with weak eyes who steps out into the brilliant sunshine and is blinded. The spiritual light is so intense that it transcends the discursive mind and blinds it. In Psalm 17, David says that God makes darkness his hiding place and covering and makes his temple in the dark waters of the clouds in the air around him. The dark waters in the clouds of the air symbolize the divine contemplative wisdom. When God brings souls close to him, they feel this darkness surrounding him as a temple in which he dwells. The loftiest light and clarity of God looks like dense darkness to the soul, as St. Paul says. And David in that same Psalm says: "Because of the brilliance of his presence clouds and cataracts passed over."

Oh, what a difficult life this can be! We live in such danger and it is so hard to find the truth! What is clear and true we experience as opaque and doubtful. We flee from what we need the most. We embrace whatever fills us with satisfaction and run after the worst thing for us, falling down with every step. What danger we live in! The light of our natural eyes is supposed to be our guide, but it is the first thing to mislead us on our journey to God. What we have to do is to keep our eyes shut and walk the path in darkness if we want to be sure where we are going and protect ourselves from the enemies of our house, which are the faculties of sense and reason.

The soul is well hidden and protected in the dark water surrounding God. That is where God lives. She is close to him there. The soul hides in the darkness and is safe from harm by other creatures. In another Psalm, David says: "You will hide them in the secret place of your face from disturbance by humanity. You will protect them in your temple from the contradiction of tongues."

This is about every sort of protection. Being hidden from humanity inside the face of God is about the way dark contemplation fortifies us against all the distractions that come from others. Receiving protection in his temple from the contradiction of tongues is about how the soul is absorbed in God's dark waters, the temple where the faculties are obscured and the soul is weaned from all desires contrary to the spirit. Some imperfections originate with other creatures. Some have their home in our very own flesh. Freed from these, the soul can authentically claim that she walks secure in the darkness.

The dark water of God fortifies and refreshes the soul from the beginning, even if it feels confusing and painful. From the beginning, the soul knows that she is powerless to do anything that could be an offense against God or to leave out anything that might be of service to him. The dark love stimulates an extraordinary vigilance and solicitude in the soul whose only concern is in pleasing her Beloved. She will ponder whether this or that thing might have upset God, turning her concerns over in her mind a thousand times. All the soul's desires, energy, and faculties have been gathered into one intention: paying homage to God. This is her pathway out of herself, out from all created things, toward the sweet and delicious union of love with God.

*"I climbed the secret ladder in disguise . . ."*

⟨⟨⟨⟩⟩⟩

# CHAPTER 17

*An explanation of how the dark*
*contemplation is secret.*

Theologians call dark contemplation "secret wisdom." St. Thomas says it is transmitted and infused into the soul through love. The communication is hidden from the faculties of sense and intellect. It is not a thing that the faculties can attain. The spirit of God penetrates the soul and aligns it with wisdom. In the Song of Songs, the bride says that the soul does not know or understand how this happens. It is not only the soul who fails to understand it. No one does. The Master who teaches the soul dwells deep inside her very substance, where neither the Fallen One, the natural senses, nor the discursive mind can reach. Secret.

The wisdom of love is not only secret within the darkness and tribulations of purification, which the soul is powerless to describe. It is just as secret afterwards, in the light of illumination, when the transmission comes with total clarity. The soul has no desire to try to put words on it, but even if she did she would not be able to find any descriptions or metaphors to express such sublime insight and such delicate spiritual feeling. The wisdom would remain perpetually unexpressed. Secret.

The wisdom is simple, sweeping, spiritual. It enters the mind naked of content, not dressed in the clothes of any sensory image. The intellect cannot form any idea or picture of it. Since it does not enter through the faculties, they cannot report on the colors of its garments. Still, the soul knows that she knows an exquisite and wondrous wisdom. She tastes it. It is like someone who sees something never seen before, nor has anyone ever seen anything like it. No matter how much he tried, he would not be able to give it a name, even if he was in the middle of fully understanding and enjoying it. If it is that difficult to describe something perceived through the senses, imagine how much harder it is to put words around what does not come through the senses! The language of God is like this. It relates to the soul intimately, transcending every sense and penetrating the spirit. It harmonizes both the inner and outer sensory capacities and silences them. Secret.

Sacred scripture reflects this ineffability. After God spoke to Jeremiah, all the Prophet could utter was, "Ah, ah, ah." Once God had appeared to Moses in the burning bush, Moses declared his interior powerlessness, saying that not only was he unable to speak of the encounter but that he could not even explore it in his imagination. Not only did he realize that the discursive mind is incapable of forming any image of what the soul understands from God but that the mind cannot be the recipient of divine knowledge at all. Secret.

The wisdom of contemplation is the language God speaks to the soul. It is the transmission of pure spirit to spirit alone. Nothing less than spirit—the senses, for instance—can perceive it. They cannot know it or describe it. They do not even want to. It transcends all words. Secret.

Some devoted souls on this journey, in awe of God, think they should tell the story of their experience to their spiritual guide, but they do not know how to describe it. In fact, they feel a tremendous aversion to talking about it, especially when the infused contemplation is so pure that the soul is hardly aware of it herself. All they can manage to say is that they are satisfied and serene, that they are aware of the presence of God, and that all is well. They can use nothing but general terms because the actual state is ineffable. It is a different matter when the soul has particular experiences like visions and raptures. These are communications that engage the participation of the senses and so they can be described in sensual terms. But pure contemplation is indescribable. Secret.

Mystical wisdom hides the soul inside itself. Sometimes it so thoroughly engulfs her in its secret abyss that the soul clearly sees herself as being carried far away from all she has ever known. She feels that she has been led to a vast wilderness which no human creature can reach—an immense, unbounded desert. The deeper and more solitary it is, the more lovely and delicious. The higher the soul is raised above the temporal world, the more profoundly hidden she feels. Secret.

The soul is so exalted by the abyss of wisdom, where she penetrates the veins of love's science, that she cannot help but compare this supreme knowledge and divine feeling against the conditions of natural creatures. She sees all the ordinary terms used in this life to deal with the things of God as being utterly inadequate. She considers it impossible to perceive and to know divine things as they are, no matter how learned and sublime the language someone might use. Only by illumination can mystical knowledge be transmitted. The soul is absorbing the truth that she cannot grasp or explain this wisdom. Secret.

It is not only because divine contemplation transcends the soul's natural capacity that it is called it secret, but also because it is the path that guides the soul to the perfection of union with the Beloved. The way the soul walks to God is through human unknowing. And she walks to him in divine ignorance. The soul cannot know the things of God in the midst of looking for them, but only once they have been found. Secret.

The Prophet Baruch says about this divine wisdom that "no one is able to know her ways or imagine her paths." And he says to God: "Your illumination lit up the whole world and the earth was moved and she trembled. Your way is in the sea, and your paths are in the many waters, and your footsteps shall not be known." The lightning of God that illumines the whole world is the enlightenment that divine contemplation awakens in the faculties of the soul. The moving and trembling of the earth is the painful purification it causes. To say that the road the soul travels to God is through the sea and that his footsteps are in the many waters and so unknowable is to say that the way to God is as hidden to the inner senses as would be footprints on the water to the outer senses. The traces God leaves on the souls he wants to bring to himself are unrecognizable. Secret.

In the Book of Job it says: "Do you perchance know the paths of the great clouds or the perfect knowledge?" This is about the way God continually exalts souls and perfects them in his wisdom. In secret.

# CHAPTER 18

*An explanation of how this secret
wisdom is a ladder.*

A thief climbs a ladder to break into the vault where treasures are stored. The soul, too, ascends the secret contemplation to plunder the riches of heaven.

The Royal Prophet [David] says: "Blessed is the one who receives your favor and help. In his heart he has prepared his ascent into the vale of tears in the appointed place. For in this way the Lord of the Law shall give blessing and they will go from virtue to virtue (step by step) and the God of gods shall be seen in Zion [Ps. 84:5-7] (he is the treasure of the fortress of Zion, which is utmost blessing)."

This secret wisdom can also be called a ladder because the same steps are used to ascend and descend. The transmissions that come through secret contemplation both raise the soul up to God and humble her to herself. On the path to God, to rise up is to drop down. She who humbles herself is exalted while she who exalts herself is humbled. God draws the soul high so that she can be submerged, and he lowers her so that she can be lifted back to him. Which is what the

Wise Man says: "Before the soul is exalted she is humbled, and before she is humbled she is exalted."

If the soul reflects on it, she will notice that she suffers innumerable ups and downs and that the prosperity she enjoys is always followed by some storm of tribulation. This pattern becomes so clear that the soul begins to wonder if the purpose of the calm is to fortify her against the stark poverty to come and if, since abundance and tranquility seem to arise from misery and torment, she is first compelled to fast before she can attend the feast. The soul never stays in one state for long. Contemplation involves continual ascending and descending until the soul arrives at quietude.

Remember: the state of perfection mirrors a perfect love of God and disregard of self. This state cannot exist without knowledge of God and self. The soul must practice both. First she is given a taste of the one: exultation. Then she experiences the other: humility. Finally, all this ascending and descending stops. The soul reaches God and attains perfect stillness. God is at the end of the ladder. The ladder rests in God. It is God that the ladder is leaning against. This is the ladder that Jacob saw in his sleep, on which angels were climbing up and down, from God to human and human to God, with God himself holding the whole thing up. Sacred scripture says that all this happened at night while Jacob slept, which expresses how secret the path to God is and how it transcends ordinary human understanding.

The ascent has to be secret to the soul. She balks at annihilation of the self. She considers it to be catastrophe, even though it is the greatest of blessings. She also thinks consolation and gratification, which create attachment and so bring only loss, are some kind of prize.

Contemplation is the science of love. It is an infused knowledge of God that both illumines and impassions the soul, drawing her upward step by step into the arms of the Beloved. The ladder of love is so secret that God alone can measure it.

———— ⬥⬥⬥ ————

# CHAPTER 19

*An explanation of the first five steps on
the mystical ladder of divine love.*

The first step on the ladder of love sickens the soul—in the very best way. The bride says in the Song of Songs: "I beseech you, daughters of Jerusalem, if you find my Beloved, tell him I am sick with love." This is not a sickness unto death. It is for the glory of God. The soul languishes in response to all that is not of God, for the sake of him alone. "My soul has swooned (away from all things) for your salvation," says David.

A sick person loses his appetite for food and his color changes. The soul on this step loses her taste for everything and the colors of her past existence are transmuted. The soul contracts this disease when excessive heat is sent from above. Once she begins to climb the ladder of contemplation, the soul quickly becomes aware of her impending annihilation. She has been rendered incapable of finding satisfaction or support in anything. There is nowhere for her to rest.

The second step on the ladder of love compels the soul to seek God ceaselessly. The bride says that she initially sought him by night in her bed. This reflects the first step, where the soul languishes in love. When she cannot find her Beloved, the bride says: "I shall rise up and seek him whom my soul loves." David says: "Seek the face of God always." The soul searches for him in all things. Nothing diverts her attention until she finds him. She resembles the bride who asks the guards about him and then rushes past them, not pausing for a response. Mary Magdalene did not even pay attention to the angels in Christ's tomb!

The soul on this step is profoundly solicitous. She is focused entirely on her Beloved. Whenever she thinks, her thoughts turn instantly to the Beloved. Whenever she is in conversation, she speaks only of him, no matter what is the topic at hand. Whether eating, sleeping, or waiting, all her care is centered on the Beloved. The soul is healing and gaining strength on this step, which propels her to the next step. Now she enters a new degree of purification in the night.

The third step on the ladder of love inspires the soul to do good work and reinforces her determination not to falter. The Royal Prophet says: "Blessed is the person in awe of God; he yearns to work hard in his commandments." If awe, a child of love, generates this fervor in the soul, what will love itself create? On this step, the soul thinks that the great work she does for the Beloved is small; her many deeds, few; the long time she spends serving him, short. It is the fire of love blazing inside her that gives her this perspective.

The intensity of Jacob's love made him think that his obligation to serve another seven years beyond the seven he

had already served was not much. If Jacob's love for a creature could have such an effect on him, what will love for the
Creator produce inside the soul on this step? In her passion
for God, the soul suffers sorrow in not being able to do all
she would wish to do for him. If she could only destroy herself a thousand times for him, it would be a comfort to her!
As it is, she considers everything she does to be worthless
and sees her life as useless. Inside herself, the soul is convinced that she is bad—worse than anyone else. This solicitude is a wondrous benefit. Love is teaching the soul how
much God deserves. How could her small efforts be worthy
of God, who is so great? The soul on this step is far removed
from pride, presumption, and the inclination to judge others. She is quietly building the courage she needs to climb to
the next step.

On the fourth step of the ladder of love, the soul experiences a persistent suffering but without accompanying weariness. As St. Augustine says, love makes all burdens light.
When the bride was on this step, yearning to skip ahead
to the end of the ladder, she called out to the Beloved: "Put
me as a seal upon your heart, as a seal upon your arm, for
love is as strong as death and reverence and supplication endure as long as hell."

The spirit has so much energy on this step that it effortlessly brings the flesh under control. Spirit pays as much attention to flesh as a tree would to one of its leaves. The soul
is not interested in consolation or satisfaction, either from
God or from anything else. She does not use prayer to ask

for favors. She realizes that God has already given her uncountable gifts. The only thing the soul cares about is how she can serve him. She would do anything to repay the God who has been so generous, no matter how high the cost to herself.

Her heart cries out: Ah, my beloved God, how many go to you looking for their own solace and satisfaction and desiring that you grant them favors and gifts, but those longing to give you pleasure and offer you something at cost to themselves, putting their own interests last, are few. What is lacking is not that you, O my God, are unwilling to grant us new favors, but our failure to use what we have already received to serve you only, and so we continually compel you to bestow your mercies upon us.

This step of love is very high. The suffering of the soul at this stage for love of God alone is so pure that he often pays her little visits of sweet spiritual delight, which bring her joy. The boundless compassion of God cannot endure the suffering of his beloved for long without responding. Jeremiah says: "I have remembered you, pitying your youth and tenderness, when you followed me into the desert." The desert represents detachment from every creature; the soul cannot rest or find refuge anywhere. This step so inflames the soul and enkindles her passion for God that it propels her up to the next level.

On the fifth step of the ladder of love, the soul is filled with impatience. Her longing to meet her Beloved and have union with him is so intense that any delay, no matter how slight, is unbearably tedious. She continually thinks that she is on the brink of finding him. When she sees her desire frustrated, which is at almost every step, she swoons in her yearning. The Psalmist says: "My soul longs and faints for the dwelling places of the Lord."

The soul on this step must either see her Beloved or die. This was the love that burned in Rachel's heart when she cried out in her longing: "Give me children or I will die." This is where souls "suffer hunger like dogs circling the City of God." It is the step of soul-hunger. It is where the soul feeds on love and is satisfied in proportion to her desire. Well fed, she has the energy to ascend to the next step.

# CHAPTER 20

*The other five steps of love.*

On the sixth step, the soul runs toward God. Her hope keeps her from fainting as she rushes to him. Energized by love, she flies swiftly. The Prophet Isaiah says: "The saints who hope in God shall renew their strength. They shall take wings like the eagle and shall not faint." The next verse of the Psalm also reflects this step: "As the deer desires the waters, so my soul desires you, O my God." When it is thirsty, the deer races to the water. The soul's charity has been exceedingly heightened and is now almost completely purified, which accelerates her pace. The Psalm says: "I ran the path of your commandments, once you expanded my heart." It does not take long for the soul to arrive at the next step.

The seventh step gives the soul a burning boldness. On this level, the soul pays no attention to the judgment that she should be patient and wait. She ignores advice to step back. She is incapable of being shamed into withdrawal. God makes her ardently daring. The Apostle says: "Charity believes all things, hopes all things and endures all things."

Moses spoke from this step when he implored God to forgive the people or else to strike his name from the Book of Life. When souls approach God joyfully, they get what they ask for. David says: "Delight in God, and he will grant you the petition of your heart." The bride became so brave on this step that she cried out: "Let him kiss me with the kiss of his mouth!"

It is not appropriate for the soul to be too bold on this step unless she distinctly feels the inner blessing of the King's scepter extended toward her. If not, she could easily tumble back down the steps she has already climbed. She must always maintain her humility. From the power of the daring and passionate love that God gives the soul on this step, she draws the energy to reach the next level. This is where the soul captures the Beloved and unites with him.

The eighth step of love impels the soul to take hold of the Beloved without letting him go. The bride says: "I found him whom my heart and soul loves; I held him and did not let him go." Although the soul satisfies her desire on this step, her satisfaction is not unbroken. Some souls attain their footing and then lose it again. Who could sustain a state of pure glory in this life? The soul can rest there for only short periods of time. God ordered the Prophet Daniel to stay on this level: "Daniel, remain on your step, because you are a man of desires."

The ninth step makes the perfected soul burn gently in love of God. St. Gregory says that when the Holy Spirit appeared to the disciples, they burned inwardly with a tender love. I can't really speak of the treasures the soul receives on this step. Even if I were to write a thousand books about them, the bulk of the truth would be left untold.

The tenth and final step on the ladder of love does not belong to this life. Through the clear vision of God that the soul attains here, she is instantly and unequivocally assimilated into him. Once she passes beyond the ninth step in this life, the soul departs from the body. St. John says: "We know that we shall be like him." It's not that the individual soul will have the capacity of God—this is impossible—but that all that she is will become like God.

And so the soul will be called, and so shall she be, God by participation.

On the highest steps of love, the secret ladder is not so secret anymore. Love generates amazing effects. Everything is revealed to the soul! On this final step of clear vision, where the soul finds God resting at the top of the ladder, she merges completely with him and nothing remains hidden from her. Christ said: "On that day, you shall ask me nothing." Until that day, no matter how high the soul climbs, something will remain secret, in proportion to her separation from the divine essence.

At last, through infused contemplation and secret love, the soul transcends herself and all things and ascends to God. Love is like a fire. It rises perpetually upward, yearning to be absorbed at its very center.

# CHAPTER 21

*An explanation of why the soul says that she is
in disguise, and a description of the colors
of the disguise the soul wears in the night.*

We disguise ourselves by hiding under a garment that makes
us look different from who we really are. We use our disguise
to please and charm our Beloved or to elude our enemy and
accomplish our mission undetected. We choose the clothing
that most clearly reflects our heart's desire and also most
carefully conceals us from discovery by those who would do
us harm.

The soul, filled with love of God and longing for his
friendship, leaves her house dressed in the vivid hues of her
affection. She goes out covered in love and she is safe, invisible to her three adversaries: the world, the animal nature,
and the Spirit of Evil. She wears garments of three different
colors: white, green, and red, which symbolize the three
virtues: faith, hope, and charity.

The inner robe of faith is pure white: radiant, blinding to
the eye of the discursive mind. It is the foundation of all the
other virtues. Clothed in faith, the soul is protected from
the Fallen One. Dressed in white, the soul captures the heart

of her Beloved and attains union with him. Without faith, says the Apostle, it is impossible to please God; with faith, he says, it is impossible not to. It is as if God were saying to the soul: If you desire union with me, come clad in faith beneath everything.

The soul was wearing the white robe of faith when she went out into the dark night and traveled the dangerous depths of inner emptiness. There was no comfort for her senses, no light for her intellect. No relief from above: God's house seemed to be locked and the Master hidden away. No relief from below: her spiritual guides had nothing left to offer. And yet the soul suffered with humility and perseverance. She passed through these troubles without growing discouraged and blaming the Beloved. The Beloved proves his lover's faith. "Because of the words of your lips, I have kept hard ways," says David.

Over the white robe of faith, the soul spreads a green shawl of hope. Draped in hope, she is liberated from her second adversary: the world. This is the green of living hope in God; it fills her heart with courage. Hope lifts the soul to the sphere of eternal life. In comparison with these divine aspirations, all earthly things seem withered and worthless. The soul cannot take back her worldly wardrobe. She can no longer focus her desire on anything that was, is, or will be in the world. She lives wrapped in hope for nothing less than the infinite. Her heart is so transported that she cannot touch earthly things. She can't even see them.

St. Paul calls this green disguise the "helmet of salvation."

A helmet protects the whole head. It covers it entirely, except for a visor to peek out of. Hope shrouds the mind's senses so that they will not become absorbed in worldly things. Shielded by hope, no arrow from the world can wound the soul. Hope opens a visor in the soul through which she can look only toward the divine. David says: "Just as the eyes of the handmaid are fixed on the hands of her mistress, so are our eyes fixed on our God until he has mercy on us who hope in him."

Wearing the luminous green shawl, gazing perpetually upon God and nothing else, content only with him, the soul brings delight to her Beloved, and he gives her all that she hopes for. Without this green shawl of hope in God alone, the soul might as well not even start out on her journey of love. It is unrelenting hope that moves and overcomes all obstacles.

As the perfect finishing touch of the disguise, the soul puts on the precious red cloak of charity. The third virtue lends elegance to the other two and lifts the soul near to God. The red cloak of charity makes the bride so alluring to her Beloved that she dares to say: "Although I am black, O daughters of Jerusalem, I am beautiful and so the king has loved me and brought me to his chamber."

The cloak of charity is a mantle of love. It heightens love for the Beloved. It protects and conceals the soul from her third adversary: the animal nature. Where there is true love of God, the urge for self-gratification and the attachment to one's own things cannot enter. Charity strengthens and revitalizes the other virtues. It renders them more genuine. It graces them with loveliness and deeply pleases God. Without charity, no other virtue touches God. The Song of Songs calls charity the seat draped in purple on which God rests.

The three-colored virtues prepare the three faculties of mind, memory, and will for union with God. Faith darkens and empties the mind of all natural understanding and so prepares it for union with divine wisdom. Hope pulls the memory away from all creature attachments. St. Paul says that hope is for that which one does not have. And so it withdraws the memory from the ordinary things that can be possessed and focuses it on the glory the soul hopes for. Charity annihilates the appetites of the will, ruining the soul's taste for anything that is not God. Charity centers the desires on God alone. Charity cultivates the will and merges it with God through love.

The virtues separate the soul from all that is less than God; their purpose is to join her with God. Unless the soul walks sincerely in these three virtues, it is impossible for her to reach perfect union with God through love. It is vital for the soul to wear this disguise if she is to reach her goal, which is sweet and loving union with the Beloved. It was a blessed chance the soul took when she put on this disguise and stayed with it until the end of her journey. That is why she cries out in the next verse:

*"O exquisite risk!"*

# CHAPTER 22

*An explanation of the third line
of the second verse.*

It was an indescribably exquisite risk for the soul to sneak away like that! She broke free from the Spirit of Evil, free from the world, and free from her own sensuality. She reached the blissful liberation everyone yearns for. She rose from the lowly to the sublime. Once earthly, she is now heavenly. Being human, she became divine. She joined the celestial conversation.

The reason I agreed to write this book is that many souls who pass through the dark night do not understand it and so their suffering is unbearable. Now, maybe the nature of the night is a little clearer. Although no descriptions could ever come close to expressing the magnitude of holiness this night brings to the soul, I have endeavored to share something of the sweetness that infuses the soul who passes through it.

Now, when a soul recoils in horror from the abundant tribulations of the dark night, she may draw some courage as she remembers that uncountable blessings come to her from these trials.

# CHAPTER 23

*An explanation of the fourth verse, which tells of the soul's wondrous hiding place during the night and shows that while the fragmented self can get into other very high places, it has no access to this one.*

The Spirit of Evil, caught in the illusion of separation, is rebelling against the impending union of the soul with God and trying to trick the soul and delude her in an effort to prevent its own annihilation. But these antics are fruitless. Darkness keeps the soul safe. Infused contemplation, which is passive and secret, has instilled unshakable security in the soul by this point on her journey. The faculties of sense and reason have nothing to do with it. The soul's path is cleared of any obstacles arising from sensual or mental weakness. Without access through the faculties, the soul is hidden from the fragmented self, which has no notion of what is truly happening inside the soul or how to reach her there. The more purely spiritual, the more deeply interior and the farther removed from the realm of senses is this divine communion, the less it can be grasped by the fragmented self.

Unhindered by sensual attachments, the soul experiences abundant freedom of spirit. Christ says: "Let not your left hand know what your right hand is doing." He means, do

not allow the left side of your being, which is the lower aspect of your nature, know what's going on with the right
side, which is your higher spiritual self. Keep this as a secret
between the spirit and God alone.

Even though the fragmented self has no place in this
deeply interior spiritual communion, the profound quietude in the senses alerts the negative forces within the soul
that great blessings are secretly unfolding. The fragmented
self does everything in its power to stir up the sensual nature
with a multitude of terrors and torments. The purpose is to
so agitate the soul that her spiritual nature is disquieted and
the flow of divine transmission interrupted.

Yet when infused contemplation opens the way for divine
communion to lay its naked siege on the soul, the spirit is
strengthened and the insidious activity of the fragmented
self is ultimately stilled. Instead of being blocked, the soul's
blessings multiply and her equanimity crystallizes. What a
beautiful thing! As soon as the soul detects the presence of
her adversary, she slips into her innermost depths. She does
not try to do this. She does not understand how it happens.
All the soul knows is that there is a hidden refuge inside of
her and that she is absolutely safe there.

The serenity and joy that the fragmented self tried to steal
from the soul only increases in this place. All her fears remain locked outside. The soul exults in clear consciousness
of boundless joy. Neither the world nor the fragmented self
can take away the sweet peace that comes from the hidden
Beloved. In the Song of Songs, the bride sings: "See how

sixty men surround the bed of Solomon because of the terrors of the night." The soul is conscious of this protection and peace at the same time that she is aware that outside the sanctuary, her flesh and bones are being tormented.

Divine communications are not always transmitted exclusively to the spirit. Sometimes the senses participate. This makes it easier for the fragmented self to gain access to the soul and terrorize her with immense and unspeakable anguish. When the naked spirit of negativity meets the naked spirit of goodness, the horror is intolerable. The bride suffered from this kind of turmoil when all she wanted was to drop down into an inner recollection of the fruits of divine blessing: "I descended to the garden of nuts to see the apples of the valley and if the vineyard was in flower. I knew nothing. My soul was troubled by the chariots (the clatter and the roaring) of Aminadab (the Spirit of Evil)."

When spiritual blessings are transmitted on the wings of the angelic self, the small self may catch their scent and try to impede the blessings. God gives the fragmented self free rein. That way, it cannot complain that it wasn't given a fair chance to conquer the soul. If God did not allow a certain parity between the good warrior and the bad warrior, the triumph of the angelic self would be hollow. As it is, the soul is victorious over temptation by the fragmented self and the reward for her faith is immeasurable.

God allows the fragmented self to act on the soul as fully and as effectively as he himself does. If the soul receives visions from the angelic self, God permits the fragmented self to offer false visions of the same kind. Unless she is vigilant, the soul can be easily deceived by their outward appearance. There is a good example of this in Exodus where it says that all the true signs Moses manifested were reproduced as illusions by Pharaoh's magicians: if he produced frogs, they did, too; if he turned water into blood, so did they.

But at this final stage of the soul's journey, the fragmented self is powerless to simulate the spiritual transmissions that are coming to her. There are no phenomenal images to imitate. The nature of the communications is formless. All the fragmented self can do is try and pretend to be the true self. It fails.

At the point where the soul says "yes" to spiritual contemplation, the fragmented self sometimes barges in and creates pandemonium before the soul can take cover and hide. Other times, the soul is quick enough to retreat before the fragmented self can make any significant impression on her. Then, in the powerful grace transmitted by the angelic self, the soul recollects her blessings.

Sometimes, though, as the soul nears the end of her path, the fragmented self momentarily prevails and envelops the soul in horror, causing her greater anguish than she has ever suffered in this life. This is a direct transmission from the purely negative to the purely positive aspects of the spirit. It bypasses the senses. It causes an unbearable, amorphous pain. The soul could never remain in the body if this spiritual suffering were to endure, and so it soon passes. But the soul carries the memory of profound violation and it brings her continued grief.

This battle unfolds passively inside the soul, without her doing anything. When the spirit of good yields to the spirit of evil, the soul is purified and prepared for the feast to come. God never destroys without giving life. He humbles the soul only to exalt her afterwards. In proportion to the dark and terrible purgation the soul has suffered, now she will enjoy the most wondrous and blissful spiritual communion—transcending all language and all concepts. The terror wrought by the fragmented self has refined the soul so purely that now she is an empty vessel, ready to receive absolute goodness. One true spiritual vision opens the way for another one, even more sublime. These visions belong more to the next life than to this one.

It is when God visits the soul through the angelic self that the soul cannot fully hide from the fragmented self. But when God touches the soul directly, she is concealed by perfect darkness and is safe. God dwells at the center of the soul, where neither the angelic self nor the fragmented self can reach. In this place, the soul and God enter into intimate communion. These spiritual communications are substantial touches of the sacred union between God and the soul. They are wholly divine. A single one of these gifts brings the soul greater good than any spiritual experience of her lifetime. This is the highest state of prayer possible.

It is the touch the bride was calling out for in the Song of Songs when she sang: "Let him kiss me with the kiss of his mouth."

All the soul has ever longed for is intimacy with God. She values the direct touch of divinity above any other blessing. In light of her yearning to meet the Beloved face-to-face, the bride is entirely unimpressed by the myriad favors she has been granted. Instead, she cries: "Who will give you to me, my brother, that I might find you alone, apart from the breasts of my mother, so that I may kiss you and no one will despise me or dare to attack me?"

This is about the divine communication God grants straight to the soul, independent of all creature-connections. The breasts of sensual attachment are empty, leaving the soul free to bask in divine blessing with intimate delight and profound peace. Only the soul that goes into spiritual hiding and surrenders to absolute nakedness and purification receives the blessed touch of God. The soul reaches this unutterable goodness in darkness and concealment. In darkness the hidden soul is fully empowered by the union of love with God.

The soul has an awareness now that her greater spiritual being is somehow detached from her smaller sensual being, but she doesn't know how this happened. The two detached aspects of the self feel to her to be so distinct that the soul cannot believe they have anything at all to do with each other. In a way, this is true. When communion is fully spiritual, the sensual self is completely uninvolved.

And so the soul becomes wholly spiritual, at last. Desires of sense and of spirit fall away in this place of unitive contemplation, which inspires the soul to sing out:

*"My house, at last, grown still."*

# CHAPTER 24

*The concluding explanation*
*of the second song.*

The house of the soul is still at last. Her higher spiritual self has laid down to rest along with her lower sensual self. All her desires and all her faculties are sleeping. She is free. She escapes into the night for her secret rendezvous with the Beloved . . .

Just as the soul has been ravaged by the battle of the dark night on both a sensual and a spiritual level, she now enjoys sensual and spiritual tranquility. The innocence of Adam is restored. Touches of divine union soothe the soul, giving her the deepest peace possible in this life. Hidden from her own fragmented self with its accompanying attachments, the soul is purified, silenced, and strengthened in readiness for ultimate union with God.

The moment the two aspects of the self are put to rest and all the members of her household fall asleep, divine wisdom enters the soul and forms a unique bond of love with her. In the Book of Wisdom, it says: "When peaceful stillness encompassed everything and the night in its course was half-spent, your omnipotent word, O God, leapt down from the divine throne." In the Song of Songs, the bride sings that after she passed by the ones who tore off her veil and wounded her, she finally found him whom her soul loved.

Only with great purity can the soul reach union. And only through radical detachment from all created things can she attain purity. Taking the bride's veil and wounding her in her search for the Beloved through the night reflects this nakedness and humility. She could not possibly put on the new bridal veil until the old one was stripped away. Remember when the bride tried to seek the Beloved in the comfort of her own bed? Until the soul surrenders her personal will and goes out into the dark night in search of God, she will not find him.

# CHAPTER 25

*A small explanation of the third verse.*

Still using the metaphor of the temporal night to describe the night of spirit, the soul sings of its excellent qualities. In discovering these qualities, the soul made good use of them and quickly attained her goal.

The first quality of the sweet night is its depth. God leads the soul to a state of contemplation so profound, so remote and alien to the senses, that nothing of a sensual nature—not any touch of any creature—can push her off the path to union.

The second quality of the sweet night is its darkness. All the faculties of the spirit are bathed in obscurity. The soul cannot see a thing. Nothing apart from God can sway her. She walks directly to him, free of any forms arising from any natural perception which might otherwise have interfered with her merging into the formless eternal being of God.

The third quality of this sweet night is its love. The soul finds no support from her discursive mind or from any external guide along her spiraling path to God. Dense darkness has deprived her of all natural satisfaction. Love alone burns in her heart, filling her with such absolute longing that it sends her soaring to God along the road of solitude in an utterly mysterious way.

What a sweet, sweet night!